Technical Merit: A History of Figure Skating Jumps

Ryan Stevens

Foreword by Donald Jackson

Canadian Cataloguing in Publication Data

Title: Technical Merit: A History of Figure Skating Jumps / Ryan Stevens, foreword by Donald Jackson
Author: Stevens, Ryan, 1982-
ISBN: 9781738198207

Copyright © 2023
by Ryan Stevens

Independently published
All rights reserved

Every reasonable effort has been made to cite and/or credit all source material included in this book. If errors or omissions have occurred, they will be corrected in future editions provided written notification and supporting documentation has been received by the author.

Cover photo: Freddie Tomlins at the 1936 Winter Olympic Games. Photo courtesy National Digital Archive, Poland.

Copyright notice: "Photographs available at www.audiovis.nac.gov.pl are public domain or the owner of the copy rights is the State Treasury, represented by the National Digital Archive which grant free of charge license for free use of the materials on all known exploitation fields."

"As a rule an author has one or two popular ways of contrasting the past with the present. He can treat the past as lying in comparative doleful ignorance, or he can explain that the past was infinitely superior to the day we live in. Of course, either method is the popular journalism of the moment, and in reality there is no sharp contrast, but a gradual transition which leads the past into the present."

– Joel B. Liberman

Table of Contents

FOREWORD..1
INTRODUCTION..3
THE WALTZ JUMP......................................6
THE SALCHOW..13
THE TOE-LOOP.......................................26
THE LOOP..41
THE FLIP..51
THE LUTZ...65
THE AXEL...77
THE WALLEY 93
SIDE-BY-SIDE JUMPS............................101
TWIST LIFTS...116
THROW JUMPS.....................................124
THE BACKFLIP......................................136
IJS FIRSTS...143
LIST OF JUMPS.....................................149
IJS JUMP BASE VALUES 164
ACKNOWLEDGMENTS..........................166
A NOTE FROM THE AUTHOR.................167
OTHER BOOKS.....................................168

Foreword

This book is a wonderful chronicle of the evolution of jumping in the sport of figure skating right from its beginnings.

Ryan Stevens has done very extensive research and his work is invaluable to the sport now and in the future.

We can all learn something about our sport from this book.

Reading about the accomplishments of the early skaters and seeing how they built on the past and how difficult the progress of jumping was, you can see the challenges in the sport but you can also imagine where it could go in the future.

I think it is important that skaters have an understanding and appreciation of the history and context of the jumps they are working on every day in training.

Thank you Ryan for providing this great resource for our sport.

Donald Jackson

World Champion
Olympic Medallist
2 time North American Champion
4 time Canadian Champion

Introduction

Lovers of skating have long had a thirst for firsts. In many cases, that simply isn't a thirst that can be quenched in the way some might like. Like it or Lutz it, history just isn't straightforward most of the time.

Technical standards have evolved over time. Before World War II, performing three turns out of a jump was the norm.

In the early days of international figure skating competitions, there was no such thing as a technical specialist scrutinizing how each jump was performed. If a skater managed to stay upright on a jump landing, they were often deemed to have executed it, whether it was 'clean' or not. The focus on clean landings is, in the grand scheme of things, a pretty recent phenomenon.

We simply can't judge the skating of years past through the lens of the IJS system; nor can we say with certainty the results of the competitions we see today would be the same under the 6.0 system.

Until live streams were first introduced in very recent years, video coverage of figure skating competitions in their entirety was a rarity. Spectators could really only assess 'who did what' based on the handful of performances that were televised.

Protocols, newspaper reports, articles in skating periodicals and handwritten notes by those who attended events in person serve as the surviving records of these competitions. The misidentification of a jump (or failure to mention it) by any of those who chronicled the event could easily mean that a skater who executed a jump for the first time wasn't credited with it, and vice versa.

In the decades before television, five different skaters from five different countries could easily have been working on the same jump at the same time. In many instances, we have no way of knowing if a skater in St. Moritz or Stockholm did such-and-such a jump combination first and guess what? That's okay.

What we absolutely can do is look back through the information that is hiding in plain sight and make attempts to trace the recorded history of figure skating jumps. That is what this book, in a very small way, aims to do. I hope you'll be interested - and maybe even a little surprised - by what you learn!

The Waltz Jump

The waltz jump takes off from the forward outside edge of the left foot, landing on the back outside edge of the other foot.

Over the years, the waltz jump has been known by many names, including the half-turn[1], flying three[2] and three jump[3].

One of the earliest written references to a waltz jump being performed comes from a French skating book called "Le Vrai Patineur, ou principes sur l'art de patiner avec grace", penned by Jean Garcin two years before Napoleon Bonaparte was sent into exile[4]. Garcin called the jump 'Le Saut de Zéphyre', likely referencing Zephyrus, the Greek God of the gentle west wind.[5] Garcin described 'Le Saut de Zéphyre' as "a compound step. It is done by an outside forward on the right foot, in the attitude of the big outside, at the end of

---

1 "Young Sportsman's Guide: Ice Skating", Michael Kirby, 1962
2 "Krasobrusleni", Vladimir Koudelka, 1946
3 "Ice Rink Skating", Captain T.D. Richardson, 1949
4 "Napoleon at St. Helena, Vol. 1", Barry Edward O'Meara, 1889
5 "Taking Shape: Finding Sculpture in the Decorative Arts", Henry Moore Institute, Leeds and J. Paul Getty Museum, Los Angeles, California, 2009

which one jumps while trying to fall on the edge of the other foot, in the pose of the back outside with arms in the place. This step can be repeated several times on the right before repeating it on the left. It [can] still be done without jumping, but although it is very pretty too, it no longer seems to be the same, so much is it less brilliant and less perilous."[6] Garcin does not claim to have invented Le Saut de Zéphyre, so it may well have been performed for some years prior.

The jump was being performed in North America by at least the 1860s. In 1868, Marvin R. Clark and Frank Swift described 'flying threes' as "a showy and particularly dashing figure... performed by starting off with the plain 'figure three' on the right foot, and from that to the left foot, and continuing the movement from one foot to the other, going lengthwise of the ice. This movement is frequently done with a jump, but it is less graceful, although more dashing, and really destroys the figure, thus: It should, therefore, be done without a jump."[7]

---

[6] "Le Vrai Patineur, ou principes sur l'art de patiner avec grace", Jean Garcin, 1813
[7] "The Skater's Text Book", Marvin R. Clark and Frank Swift, 1868

In 1881, a group of European disciples of Jackson Haines published a textbook on the Viennese school of skating called "Spuren auf dem Eis"[8]. Demeter Diamantidi, Carl von Korper Marienwerth and Max Wirth attributed a polka-mazurka ice dance that included a small jump attributed to Haines. The authors praised a jump they called the 'Überspringen Des Dreier', which translates loosely to 'skipping the three'. The authors wrote: "An interesting field for the bold jumper is the skipping of the half-turns... which has experienced a notable increase through the wrong turns of threes and alternations. If one considers all these figures, there are 16 different types of jumps. If one adds those which result from jumping the three from one foot to the other, the number of jumps increases to 20... Skipping the three is a figure of surprising effect when performed correctly. The skipping takes place after a few outside edge runs with one skater forward and the other backwards in that the one who skates the forward outside jumps over the three from the one foot to the other and thus the forward outside goes to the

---

[8] "Spuren auf dem Eis", Demeter Diamantidi, Carl von Korper Marienwerth and Max Wirth, 1881

reverse arc. The person who is skipping must be offered help by the person originally skating backwards... and outwards in such a way that he is lifted as high as possible during the jump and supported until his foot is safely on the ice again. Landing on both feet is incorrect." The novel way of doing (assisted) waltz jumps the authors described was really a precursor to pairs skating, not singles skating.

While most young skaters today learn the waltz jump first, then the Salchow or toe-loop, loop, flip, Lutz and Axel, it's important to recognize that in the very early stages of international figure skating competitions, very little importance was really played to jumps or the order they were learned in. Free skating performances consisted mostly of spirals, toe-spins, pivots, footwork and figures – both compulsory and 'special' figures[9] of the skater's own design. The odd jump was peppered among these as a highlight by most, but not all, skaters.[10] In 1908, Edgar and Madge Syers suggested the following jumps to those crafting a free skating program: "A plain

---
9 "The Art of Skating: International Style", Madge and Edgar Syers, 1913
10 "Kunstfertigkeit im Eislaufen", Robert Holletschek, 1925

jump which replaces the skater on a continuation of the same edge on the same foot, or a Counter or Rocker jump from FO to BO, or FI to BI. A high jump is more effective than a long one, the skater must be careful to maintain a good position, the legs not being tucked up, the return to the ice as light and quiet as possible." They did not specifically mention a waltz jump in their book, though they did incidentally mention a more difficult loop jump.[11]

Incidentally, most early skating literature doesn't even bring up a waltz jump. The two kinds of jumps that were most frequently mentioned were E.T. Goodrich's signature[12] spread eagle jump "executed while the skater is under considerable headway in the 'Spread Eagle' movement [jumping] clear from the ice, making a complete revolution in the air, and alights in the same position of the start"[13] and high and long jumps. Tibor von Földváry of Hungary and Eduard Engelmann Jr. of Austria were two of the first skaters to do the spread eagle jump - known as the Mondsprung or

---

11 "The Book of Winter Sports", Madge and Edgar Syers, 1908
12 "The Skater's Text Book", Marvin R. Clark and Frank Swift, 1868
13 "A Guide to Artistic Skating", George Meagher, 1919

Moon Jump[14] in Europe - in international competition during the Victorian era.[15]

Early skating clubs required skaters to jump over obstacles, such as stacked hats, to gain admission.[16] It has been speculated that this was a way of discouraging weaker skaters, but such feats may initially have been more practical than showy. Demeter Diamantidi, Carl von Korper Marienwerth and Max Wirth noted that high and long jumping on ice was already quite common by the 1880's. Skaters practiced these jumps so that in the event of a crack in the ice occurring, they were prepared to 'jump to safety'. By 1881, Viennese skaters "had made it to a 10-foot long jump."[17]

High and long jumps became the backbone of a whole other 'genre' of skating called barrel jumping[18], which in one form or another became an absolute staple in the professional

---

14 "Das Eissport-Buch", Fritz Reuel, 1928
15 "Theorie und Praxis des Kunstlaufes am Eise", Gilbert Fuchs, 1926
16 "The Edinburgh Skating Club with Diagrams of Figures and List of the Members", William Grant, 1865
17 "Spuren auf dem Eis", Demeter Diamantidi, Carl von Korper Marienwerth, Max Wirth, 1881
18 "It Happened in the Catskills", Harvey and Myrna Katz Frommer, 1991

ice show world for decades. The humble waltz jump - or Le Saut de Zéphyre or Überspringen Des Dreier if you will – became the stepping stone to all of the other jumps you will read about in this book.

The Salchow

The Salchow is a full-revolution jump from the back inside edge of one foot to the back outside edge of the other.

The jump is the namesake of Sweden's Ulrich Salchow, who won the first Olympic gold medal in men's figure skating in 1908, in addition to ten World titles between the years 1901 and 1911.

For many years, it has been stated that Ulrich Salchow first performed his jump in 1909[19] or 1910[20], after he won his Olympic gold medal. His wife Anna Elisabeth (Bahnson) Salchow[21] asserted that he had actually developed the jump much earlier, in preparation for the 1900 World Championships in Davos.[22]

---

19 "Figure Skating", Encyclopedia Britannica; "Figure Skating's Greatest Stars", Steve Milton 2009, etc.
20 "The Official Book of Figure Skating", United States Figure Skating Association, 1998
21 "Publicistklubbens porträttmatrikel", Publicistklubbens Förlag, 1936
22 "Die Dame mit der Halskette", M. Hönel, "Junge Welt", February 6, 1985; "Stilwandel im Eiskunstlauf: Eine Ästhetik- und Kulturgeschichte: Eine Ästhetik- und Kulturgeschichte", Dr. Matthias Hampe, 1994

There is considerable evidence that Ulrich Salchow was performing his jump throughout the Edwardian era. He executed three different small jumps in an exhibition he gave in Davos in January of 1903, the first being a ROF-ROB rocker jump and the second a jump from LOB-RIF. The third jump he performed was described as "once back and jump, a complete revolution in the air."[23] Two years later, he was praised for "introducing surprising jumps"[24] in his free skating performance in the World Championships for men, held as part of the Nordiska Spelen (Nordic Games) in Stockholm. A third clue is a jump described as a 'brille' of the author's invention in the 1906 edition of Salchow's own book "Handbok i konståkning på skridskor". The diagram included with the 'hop' appears to depict a three turn entry[25].

One of the possible reasons why the 1909 date has stuck as the year the Salchow jump was invented was likely the fact that the jump was described in telegrams sent

---

23 "A Handbook of Figure Skating Arranged For Use On The Ice", George Henry Browne, 1907
24 "The Figure Skating Championship", "The Field, The Country Gentleman's Newspaper", February 11, 1905
25 "Handbok i konståkning på skridskor", Ulrich Salchow, 1906

internationally in 1909 to advertise the Internationalen Kunstlaufen des Berliner Schlittschuhklubs in Berlin and 1909 World Championships in Stockholm.[26]

Ulrich Salchow stressed the need for a well-balanced free skating program, including at least two or three different figures spaced through the performance, as well as up to four different jumps and spins. However, ISU Historian Benjamin T. Wright recalled, "The irony of Salchow is the jump is what he is remembered for. He was not a good free skater. He was far better as a figure skater and what he was really well known for in his day was the Salchow rocker, which is the form of rocker in which you put the foot behind after the turn."[27]

The cancellation of ISU Championships during The Great War didn't slow the spread of the jump's popularity internationally. In 1917, the Salchow was performed by German skater Margarete Klebe in an international

---

[26] "Deutscher Wintersport", 1908/1909, "Stilwandel im Eiskunstlauf: Eine Ästhetik- und Kulturgeschichte: Eine Ästhetik- und Kulturgeschichte", Dr. Matthias Hampe, 1994
[27] "ISU: 100 Years Of Skating 1892-1992"

women's competition held in Vienna.[28]

At the 1928 Winter Olympic Games in St. Moritz, Sweden's Gillis Grafström and Canada's Montgomery Wilson made history as the first two skaters to perform a double Salchow jump in a major international competition.[29] Wilson also executed the jump in his winning performance at the 1929 North American Championships in Boston[30].

Maribel Vinson Owen recorded that "for a long while Evelyn Chandler was the only girl to do a double Salchow, though certain men could bring it off quite regularly"[31]. Cecilia Colledge had a double Salchow in her program as early as 1935[32] and Megan Taylor was praised for including double jumps in her program at the 1936 World Championships[33]. Barbara Ann Scott included

---

28 "Die Genese des Eiskunstlaufens als Prozess der Versportung und struktureller Veränderungen im Wettkampfsystem sowie der Leistungsentwicklung", Dr. Matthias Hampe, Humanwissenschaftlichen Fakultät der Universität Potsdam, 2010
29 Ibid
30 "Impressions: North American Championships", Norman V.S. Gregory, "Skating" magazine, May 1929
31 "Maribel Y. Vinson's Advanced Figure Skating", Maribel Vinson Owen, 1940
32 "A Trans-Atlantic View of Recent European Activities", Maribel Vinson, "Skating" magazine, March 1935
33 "1936 Championships of the World", Theresa Weld Blanchard,

a double Salchow jump in her program in the junior women's event at the 1940 Canadian Championships[34], eight years before winning Olympic gold.

The history of the triple Salchow may well be able to be traced back to the late 1930s. Canadian-born Lloyd 'Skippy' Baxter claimed to have performed the first triple Salchow in a competition in Los Angeles, California in 1939.[35] His achievement was the subject of one of Robert Ripley's "Believe it or Not" cartoons.[36] A report on the 1939 Pacific Coast Championships in Los Angeles in "Skating" magazine praised Baxter's split Lutz jump and double loop but unfortunately failed to mention an attempt at the triple Salchow.[37] However, newspaper articles and his biographies in show programs from the 1940s[38] indeed did recognize him as "the only known skater who can make three complete

---
"Skating" magazine, April 1936
34 "The Canadian Championships", Joan Parkins, "Skating" magazine, March 1940
35 Interview with Keri Pickett for "The Fabulous Ice Age" documentary, shared in 2013
36 "'Skippy' Baxter An Inspiration on Ice", Chris Smith, "The Press Democrat", December 19, 2012
37 Pacific Coast Championships, Pauline K. Newman, "Skating" magazine", April 1939
38 "Cool Hero", "Daily News" (New York, NY), July 17, 1942

turns in the air before landing on the ice."[39] Baxter was inducted to both the U.S. Figure Skating Hall of Fame and Professional Skaters Association Hall of Fame and was recognized by both[40] for his pioneering achievement as a 'triple jumper'.

The triple Salchow made its first appearance at an ISU Championship in 1955 when Ronnie Robertson performed both the Salchow and a triple loop[41] in his free skating performance at the World Championships in Vienna. At the U.S. Championships that followed in Colorado Springs, David Jenkins repeated Robertson's feat – landing a triple Salchow and loop of his own.[42]

By the time the 1950s were over, Donald Jackson[43] of Canada, Nobuo Sato[44] of Japan

---

39 "Who's Who on the Ice", Programme for "Howdy Mr. Ice" at the Centre Theatre, 1948
40 "U.S. Hall of Fame Presents Class of 2003", United States Figure Skating Association; "Skippy Baxter", PSA Coaches Hall of Fame biography
41 "King of the Ice", Independent (Long Beach, California), October 30, 1955
42 "United States Championships", T.O. Johnston, "Skating" magazine, June 1955
43 "The North American Championships", S.L. Rodway, "Skating" magazine, April 1959
44 "Impressions of Japanese Skating", Hank Beatty, "Skating" magazine, June 1958

and Robin Jones of the UK[45] had also performed triple Salchows in competition.

In the early 1960s, a small group of women started attempting triple Salchows in competition. Czechoslovakia's Jana Mrázková was most likely the first to attempt it, in her free skate at the 1960 Winter Olympic Games in Squaw Valley.[46] Mrázková and Austria's Helli Sengstschmid were both credited with landing the jump at the 1961 European Championships in Berlin[47], however, these claims have to be called into question. Mrázková did not even attempt the jump in Berlin[48] and although she stood up on the jump several times, her landings were not what we would today call clean – in fact, they were quite short on rotation. Dennis L. Bird was convinced that Sengstschmid landed the jump at this event, so she likely stood up on it, but her technique on doubles called into question her ability to do a clean triple.[49]

---

45 "The British Championships", Dennis L. Bird (under pseudonym John Noel), "Skating" magazine, February 1960
46 Interview with Frazer Ormondroyd, January 4, 2023; Video footage
47 "The European Championships", Dennis L. Bird (under pseudonym John Noel), "Skating" magazine, May 1961
48 Interview with Frazer Ormondroyd, January 4, 2023; Video footage
49 Ibid

German skating historian Dr. Matthias Hampe asserted that Sengstschmid had thirteen double jumps in her program, but was never successful at doing a triple.[50]

Petra Burka's triple Salchow at the 1962 Canadian Championships in Toronto was believed to be the first by a girl in figure skating history."[51] At the time, she recalled, the double Axel was seen as the limit for women's skaters and triple jumps were considered "unladylike". Petra's mother and coach Mrs. Ellen Burka remarked in 1962, "Petra has always been a natural skater. She was never taught how to do jumps, she just did them. A year ago she told me she was going to try a triple Salchow. Then she just went out on the ice, did the jump and landed it."[52] By 1963, sportswriters were claiming that she was "the first girl ever to jump the triple Salchow."[53] The Ontario Sports Hall of Fame and Canada's Sports Hall of Fame credit Burka as the first

---

50 "Die Genese des Eiskunstlaufens als Prozess der Versportung und struktureller Veränderungen im Wettkampfsystem sowie der Leistungsentwicklung", Dr. Matthias Hampe, Humanwissenschaftlichen Fakultät der Universität Potsdam, 2010
51 "Petra gunning for gold medal", "The Leader-Post" (Regina, Saskatchewan), March 9, 1962
52 Ibid
53 "Petra's burning ambition is to win Olympic medal", Winnipeg Evening Tribune, August 15, 1963

woman to land a triple jump in competition.

To further complicate matters, NSA Historian Dennis L. Bird noted that a fourth skater, Japan's Miwa Fukuhara, landed a triple Salchow in her free skating performance at the 1963 World Championships in Cortina d'Ampezzo.[54] Her attempt at the following year's World Championships in Dortmund reveals that her attempt was under-rotated[55] Sandra Stevenson believed that the first woman to do a clean triple Salchow at the World Championships was East Germany's Sonja Morgenstern, at the 1971 World Championships in Lyon, France.[56] Video footage of Morgenstern's triple Salchow at that year's European Championships shows that the jump was clean as a whistle.[57]

The fact that there has been much debate over the years over which woman did a triple Salchow first over the years boils down to the fact that some attempts which were not what we'd call 'clean' today were credited as firsts

---

54 "Arctic Cold Chills World Championships", Dennis L. Bird (under pseudonym John Noel), "Skating" magazine, May 1963
55 Interview with Frazer Ormondroyd, January 4, 2023; Video footage
56 "The BBC Book of Skating", Sandra Stevenson, 1984
57 Video footage

by the press in the countries of the respective skaters. Technical specialists and slow-motion replay weren't things and the ISU had no set process for ratifying jumps in those days. Vern Taylor's triple Axel in 1978, which will be discussed in a later chapter, was only recognized as a first because television analyst Johnny Esaw took the initiative to bring tape to the ISU for verification.[58]

Donald Jackson quietly worked on a quad Salchow jump in the 1960s. In an interview with Allison Manley on The Manleywoman SkateCast, he recalled, "I was working on quad Salchows in 1962 with Mr. Galbraith, after I turned professional, and I had it with a little cheat. I certainly would have wanted to try it if I had stayed in."[59]

Skaters didn't start attempting quad Salchows in competition until the early 1990s. France's Surya Bonaly fell on an attempt in her free skate at the 1990 European Championships in Leningrad and the 1992 World

---

[58] "Vern Taylor back where he started," Mark Brender, "The Record" (Sherbrooke, QC), December 3, 1993
[59] Interview with Donald Jackson, The Manleywoman SkateCast, November 28, 2013

Championships in Oakland[60]. American skater Michael Chack under-rotated and two-footed an attempt at the 1991 U.S. Championships in Minnesota[61]. By 1992, Kurt Browning[62], Elvis Stojko[63] and Todd Eldredge[64] had all worked on quad Salchows in practice.

In March of 1998, America's Timothy Goebel made history as the first skater to land a quad Salchow in competition at the Junior Champions Series Final (now termed the ISU Junior Grand Prix Final) in Lausanne, Switzerland[65]. Seventeen-year-old Goebel, a student of 1960 Olympic Gold Medallist Carol Heiss Jenkins, performed the jump in combination with a double toe-loop. Thus, he made history a second time as the first skater to land a quad Salchow combination in an international competition. Referee Sally-Anne Stapleford was the one responsible for confirming that he had landed the jump cleanly[66].

---

60 Video footage
61 Ibid
62 "World champion cuts Lutz from programs", Cam Cole, "Edmonton Journal", March 13, 1991
63 "Skate Canada", Gerri Walbert, "Skating" magazine, January 1992
64 "Eldredge on Eldredge", "Skating" magazine, June 1991
65 "Goebel Makes History", "American Skating World" periodical, April 1998
66 "Competition: 1998 ISU Junior Series Final", Klaus Reinhold

The first woman to successfully land a quad Salchow in international competition was Japan's Miki Ando, at the ISU Junior Grand Prix Final in The Hague in December of 2002[67].

A quad Salchow successfully landed again by a woman in international competition until March of 2018, when Russia's Alexandra Trusova performed the jump at the World Junior Championships in Sofia, Bulgaria[68]. She earned a positive GOE of 2.00, in addition to a Base Value of 10.50, for the jump[69].

The first woman to land a quad Salchow at the Winter Olympic Games was Russia's Kamila Valieva[70], in the team event at the 2022 Winter Olympics in Beijing. Valieva quickly found herself in the epicenter of the biggest international doping scandal in the history of figure skating[71], resulting in no

---

Kany, "Skating" magazine, April 1998
67 "Ice Breakers", "Skating" magazine, February 2003
68 "13-Year-Old Russian Figure Skater Makes History by Landing 2 Quads in a Routine", Sputnik International, March 11, 2018
69 Protocols, ISU World Junior Figure Skating Championships 2018, Junior Ladies Free Skating
70 "At 15, Kamila Valieva just became the 1st woman to land a quad in Olympic history", Nell Clark, NPR, February 7, 2022
71 "Kamila Valieva's sample included three substances sometimes used to help the heart. Only one is banned.", Tariq Panja, "The

medals being awarded in the team event at those Games.[72]

New York Times", February 15, 2022 (updated February 19, 2022)
72 "IOC: No medal ceremony for team event, or women's singles if Valieva is top three", NBC Olympics, February 14, 2022 (updated February 15, 2022)

The Toe-Loop

I think it goes without saying that in the early twentieth century, figure skating didn't have the same obsession with jumping as it does today. A successful skater possessed a strong mastery of the school figures and in free skating aspired only to present a charming program peppered with novel moves - a toe-pirouette here, a special figure there, maybe a spiral, pose or small jump to accentuate a highlight in the rink side orchestra's music. Jumps were by and large experiments.

One such 'experiment' was the toe-loop jump, a toe-assisted jump that takes off and lands from the back outside edge of the same foot. The toe-loop has often been credited to Bruce Mapes[73], a talented professional skater married to the famous ice show star Evelyn Chandler[74]. It is important to bear in mind that in the era of Prohibition and the Great Depression - when Mapes would have likely been including the jump in show numbers -

---

73 "Sports Illustrated Figure Skating: Championship Techniques", John 'Misha' Petkevich, 1988
74 "Bruce Mapes Sr., Dies: Former Professional Skater with 'Ice Follies' was 59", "The New York Times", February 20, 1961

skaters relied on letters, telegrams and word of mouth to communicate innovations in the sport. They didn't have smartphones they could post their new tricks on Instagram with. It's certainly possible that another skater in another part of the world was working on the same jump at the same time he was.

Going back through primary sources, you really don't see mentions of the term 'toe-loop' until the early 1940s. Skating coach Clarence Hislop described the jump, in a collection of more obscure jumps like the Bowhill and Back Inside Choctaw Jump, in an article that appeared in "Skating" magazine in January of 1944[75]. However, he didn't credit its invention to anyone.

Three years earlier, Maribel Vinson Owen had termed the leap simply as an 'outside back toe-point jump'[76]. She wrote, "Some of the most breath-taking jumps I have ever seen have been simple ones done superbly well. [An] excellent example... is my husband's OB toe-point jump, an elementary jump which is one of the first every beginner learns. Yet Guy

---

75 "Another Collection of Jumps", "Skating" magazine, January 1944
76 "Maribel Y. Vinson's Advanced Figure Skating", Maribel Vinson Owen, 1940

[Owen] removes it from the beginner's class by rising it sometimes as high as three feet off the ice and hanging suspended in mid-air for several seconds."

Roller skaters called the jump the Mapes[77] and it enjoyed far more popularity on rollers in its infancy than on the ice. In fact, many skating textbooks published in the fifties talk about double Salchow, loop, flip, Lutz and Axel jumps but omit the toe-loop entirely. In Canada and UK, it was for many years called a cherry flip[78]; in Germany the Tipp-Rittberger[79]. Others still called it a tap-loop[80], toe spin loop[81] or a Charlie[82].

When Donald Jackson won the World Championships in 1962, a double toe-loop he performed late in his program was a mere embellishment to the effortless triple Lutz and

---

77 "The Complete Book of Roller Skating", Ann-Victoria Phillips, 1979
78 "Ice Skating", Howard Bass, 1980
79 "Eiskunstlaufen eine Einführung", Freimut Stein, 1966
80 "Basic Ice Skating Skills: An Official Handbook Prepared for the United States Figure Skating Association", Robert S. Ogilvie, 1968
81 "6000 Cheer Figure Skaters in Arena Event; Mrs. Secord and Miss Prantell Sparkle", "The Philadelphia Inquirer", February 2, 1936
82 "XI Olympic Winter Games", Kikuko Minami, "Skating" magazine, April 1972

triple Salchow he'd already performed.[83] Hershey, Pennsylvania's Tommy Litz brought the toe-loop to center stage the following year, landing a triple in his free skating performance[84] at the 1963 U.S. Championships in California. British journalist Dennis L. Bird noted that Litz was the first skater to land a triple toe-loop at the Winter Olympics, in 1964[85]. He also landed the jump at that year's World Championships in Dortmund.[86]

In the decade that followed, the triple toe-loop seemed to catch on like wildfire. In 1966, David McGillvray landed the jump in the junior men's event[87] at the Canadian Championships. The following year, he landed it in the senior men's event[88], but finished fourth overall. The next two Olympic Gold Medallists, Austria's Wolfgang Schwarz[89] and

---

83 Video footage
84 "Litz Captures U.S. Figure Skate Title", "Oakland Tribune", February 10, 1963
85 Handwritten notes of Dennis L. Bird from the 1964 Winter Olympic Games, British Ice Skating archives
86 "A Spectator's Guide to Figure Skating", Debbi Wilkes, 1997
87 "These Were The Championships That Were In Peterborough, Ontario Canada", Brian Pound, "Skating" magazine, April 1966
88 "1967 Canadian Championships", Brian Pound, "Skating" magazine, April 1967
89 "Title Holders Defy Vienna Wind & Rain", Howard Bass, "Winter Sports" magazine, May 1967

Czechoslovakia's Ondrej Nepela[90], had the triple toe-loop in their arsenal, as did Tim Wood[91], the Olympic Silver Medallist in 1968 and World Champion in 1969 and 1970. At the 1976 Canadian Championships, Canada's Ron Shaver opened his program with a rare feat - a sequence of three triple toe-loops in a row[92].

In the mid-1960s, Canada's Linda Carbonetto landed both triple toe-loops and Salchows in practice, but never included the toe-loop in her program. She recalled, "They were never consistent but I could do them."[93]

American women, including Janet Lynn[94] and Melissa Militano[95], started dabbling with triple toe-loops in the late 1960s and early 1970s. Tina Noyes reportedly landed "an honest-to-goodness triple jump (toe-loop)" at the 1969 North American Championships in Colorado Springs. One woman on the judging panel still gave her a 5.1, "bringing boos and cries of

---

90 Video footage
91 Ibid
92 "Canadians", Betty Ann Bagley, "Skating" magazine, March 1976
93 Interview with Linda Carbonetto Villella, January 11, 2021
94 Video footage
95 "U.S. Championships", Jeanne R. Paul, "Skating" magazine, April 1970

'Throw her out!' from some throats."[96] Militano was reported to have landed the jump in her free skate in the junior women's event at the U.S. Championships in 1971.[97]

The first woman to land a triple toe-loop at an ISU Championship was Christine Errath, at the 1974 European Championships in Zagreb, then part of Yugoslavia.[98] Errath was also the first woman to attempt the jump at the World Championships that year, though she was unsuccessful, and the first to do the jump in combination at the 1975 European Championships in Copenhagen, Denmark.[99]

By the 1976 Olympic season, a small handful of women, including Errath, Dianne de Leeuw and Elena Vodorezova, were having success with the jump in competition. The first World Champion to include a triple toe-loop in her winning program in the women's event was Linda Fratianne in 1977.[100]

As triple toe-loops became 'a thing' in the late

---

96 Clipping from "The Oakland Californian", February 8, 1969
97 "Nationals", Virginia K. Burnham, "Skating" magazine, April 1971
98 Interview with Frazer Ormondroyd, January 4, 2023; Video footage
99 "The Illustrated Encyclopedia of Ice Skating", Mark Heller, 1979
100 Video footage

1960s and early 1970s, there came to be a decidedly American preoccupation[101] with the toe-loop and its variation, the toe-Walley[102], which was first landed by a Canadian as a triple in international competition at the 1966 World Championships and 1967 North American Championships[103] by Jay Humphry.[104]

The difference, one was told, was in the entrance and that the toe-Walley took off from an inside edge, not an outside one. This became a talking point when Elaine Zayak won the 1982 World Championships with six triple jumps - all toe-loops, Salchows and toe-Walleys - and the infamous 'Zayak rule' came into play[105]. In 1983, Alexandra Stevenson wrote, "There may be quite a controversy over triple toe-Walleys this year. For a right-footed jumper, a toe-Walley is a jump from a right inside edge and the left toe, turning counter-clockwise. The trouble is that after the approach, a left three turn, almost no one

---

101 "The BBC Book of Skating", Sandra Stevenson, 1984
102 "Webster's Sports Dictionary", G. & C. Merriam, 1976
103 Interview with Jay Humphry, January 11, 2021
104 "World Championships", Dennis L. Bird (writing under the pseudonym John Noel), "Skating World" magazine, April 1966
105 "Zayak continues to raise the bar", Elizabeth Leamy, "Skating" magazine, October 2007

steps onto the inside edge. They step onto the outside edge. That makes the jump a toe-loop jump. The new regulations state that a triple jump cannot be repeated except that one triple can be repeated in combination. At Skate America, Cynthia Coull of Canada did a triple toe-loop, a triple toe-loop in combination and a triple toe-Walley. How can the judges tell if it's a true triple toe-Walley? Most skaters are playing it safe and not trying it. Cynthia's coach, Kerry Leitch, says he has talked to many judges who say the toe-Walley can be accepted as a separate triple, but I know of many who won't. It will be interesting to see what this quarrel brings up internationally."[106] The fact that slow-mo replay was not something that ISU judges had access to under the 6.0 system is something definitely worth considering.

In the early 1980s, Donald Jackson proved that age was just a number, learning the triple toe-loop at the age of forty-two. He recalled, "On a practice session, I saw some Japanese skaters doing them at the Cricket Club working with Sheldon Galbraith. I tried it and

---
106 "International Chit-Chat", Alexandra Stevenson, "Tracings" magazine, New Englands Issue Vol. VIII, No. 7, 1983

was able to do it. I never even thought of it when I was competing. In my amateur career the only time I saw what other top level skaters were doing before I got to Worlds, was at the North American Championships, and there was no TV coverage until 1962. So there were very few examples to inspire us to increase our repertoire as skaters."[107]

In 1983, Alexandr Fadeev of the Soviet Union made history as the first skater to attempt a quad toe-loop in an ISU Championship[108], two-footing the landing and putting a hand down.[109] A year later, he made history again with an attempt at the Winter Olympic Games in Sarajevo. He under-rotated the jump and landed on two feet.[110] In 1986 at the European Championships in Copenhagen, Denmark, the ISU ruled not to ratify Jozef Sabovčík's quad toe-loop.[111] ISU Official Josef Dědič credited Kurt Browning as the first man to officially land the jump two years later at

---

107 Interview with Donald Jackson, January 3, 2023
108 "Die Genese des Eiskunstlaufens als Prozess der Versportung und struktureller Veränderungen im Wettkampfsystem sowie der Leistungsentwicklung", Dr. Matthias Hampe, Humanwissenschaftlichen Fakultät der Universität Potsdam, 2010
109 Video footage
110 Ibid
111 Interview with Jozef Sabovčík, The Manleywoman SkateCast, December 21, 2008

the 1988 World Championships in Budapest.[112]

The following year, Jozef Sabovčík's teammate Petr Barna became the first European to land a ratified quad at the Nation's Cup in Gelsenkirchen, West Germany.[113] Sabovčík had his redemption in 1995, when he made history as the first skater to land the jump in professional competition at the Men's Outdoor Championships in Sun Valley, defeating Barna.[114]

Kurt Browning's big moment in 1988 was a game-changing moment for figure skating, but it was also a personally satisfying one for Browning. The first time he attempted the jump in a public practice at the Nebelhorn Trophy in Oberstdorf in August of 1986, he tumbled. He missed the quad at Skate Canada in 1987 and the 1988 Winter Olympic Games in Calgary. He had been landing the jump in practice at the Royal Glenora Club in Edmonton since 1986[115] and told a "Toronto

---

112 "Canadian's quad jump steals world skating spotlight", Mary Hynes, "The Globe and Mail", March 26, 1988
113 "Barna becomes second to land quadruple jump", Beverley Smith, "The Globe and Mail", November 18, 1989
114 Video footage
115 "Memory Lane", The Kurt Files, Tina Tyan

Star" reporter in 1987, "When I practice really well, to have some fun at the end, I try a quad. I'm getting pretty confident with it."[116] What started as "some fun" became a serious personal goal for Browning and when he achieved it, people started thinking differently about quads... and toe-loops.

Thanks largely to Kurt Browning's teammate Elvis Stojko, who landed the first quad/double[117] and quad/triple[118] combinations in international competition, quad toe-loops became the name of the game in men's figure skating by the late 1990s. Evgeni Plushenko upped the ante at the 2002 Cup of Russia in Moscow, landing a quad toe-loop/triple toe-loop/triple loop combination.[119]

Surya Bonaly was the first woman to attempt a quadruple toe-loop in an ISU

---

116 "Quad leap a hot item for skaters", Frank Orr, "Toronto Star", October 29, 1987
117 "Third skating gold for Browning; Duchesnays in contention for victory in dance event", Cam Cole, "The Montreal Gazette", March 15, 1991
118 Video footage
119 "Die Genese des Eiskunstlaufens als Prozess der Versportung und struktureller Veränderungen im Wettkampfsystem sowie der Leistungsentwicklung", Dr. Matthias Hampe, Humanwissenschaftlichen Fakultät der Universität Potsdam, 2010

Championship, at the 1991 World Championships in Munich. Though unsuccessful, she was an important pioneer in terms of introducing quads to women's figure skating. German skating historian Dr. Matthias Hampe noted, "Technical imperfections such as edge errors, jumps from a standing position, aborted exits, tapped landings or landings that were not executed completely backwards ensured that Surya Bonaly's quadruple jump attempts were not recognized. Although she was the first woman in the world to stand a quadruple toe loop at the 1991 World Cup, she was unable to land backwards. Already at the [1990] European Championships in St. Petersburg, she dared to do quadruple toe-loops and Salchows... From 1993, she focused on combinations of two triple jumps instead of the quadruple jumps. At the 1993 World Cup, she was the first woman to succeed in the triple toe-loop/Euler/triple Salchow sequence. In 1994, the combination triple Salchow/triple toe-loop followed at the European Championships. In the 1994 Olympic competition, for the first time she offered three triple/triple combinations by a lady: toe-loop/toe-loop, toe-loop/Euler/Salchow and flip/toe-loop."[120]

Ultimately, it took almost thirty years after Surya Bonaly's first attempt at the quad toe-loop for a woman to successfully the land the jump in competition. In 2018, Alexandra Trusova of Russia was credited as the first woman to land the jump in an ISU Championship[121].

TECHNICAL FIRSTS UNDER THE IJS SYSTEM

Only jumps receiving a 0 or positive GOE were considered when compiling this data.

Triple toe-loop (men)

OLYMPICS: Jeffrey Buttle, Sergei Davydov, Anton Kovalevski, Stefan Lindemann, Evan Lysacek, Viktor Pfeifer, Evgeni Plushenko, Emanuel Sandhu, Matt Savoie, Shawn Sawyer, Zoltán Tóth, Kevin van der Perren, Tomáš Verner, Johnny Weir, Min Zhang (2006, short program)
WORLDS: Kristoffer Berntsson, Gheorghe Chiper, Samuel Contesti, Yon Garcia, Brian Joubert, Maciej Kuś,

---

120 "Die Genese des Eiskunstlaufens als Prozess der Versportung und struktureller Veränderungen im Wettkampfsystem sowie der Leistungsentwicklung", Dr. Matthias Hampe, Humanwissenschaftlichen Fakultät der Universität Potsdam, 2010
121 "Quad-o-mania: An overview of the quad jumps' history", International Skating Union, February 2022

Stéphane Lambiel, Viktor Pfeifer, Roman Serov, Silvio Smalun, Kevin van der Perren, Min Zhang (2005, Qualifying Group B)
EUROPEANS: Gheorghe Chiper, Andrei Griazev, John Hamer, Stéphane Lambiel, Viktor Pfeifer, Roman Serov, Kevin van der Perren (2005, short program)
FOUR CONTINENTS: Sean Carlow, Gareth Echardt, Ben Ferreira, Kazumi Kishimoto, Chengjiang Li, Justin Pietersen, Matt Savoie, Shawn Sawyer, Daisuke Takahashi, Min Zhang (2005, short program)

Triple toe-loop (women)

OLYMPICS: Silvia Fontana, Tuğba Karademir, Fleur Maxwell (2006, short program)
WORLDS: Miki Ando, Joanne Carter, Sasha Cohen, Idora Hegel, Lina Johansson, Yan Liu, Susanna Pöykiö, Joannie Rochette, Júlia Sebestyén (2005, Qualifying Group B)
EUROPEANS: Candice Didier, Laura Fernández, Carolina Kostner, Lina Johansson, Karen Venhuizen (2005, short program)
FOUR CONTINENTS: Amber Corwin, Na Hou, Yukari Nakano (2005, short program)

Quad toe-loop (men)

OLYMPICS: Evgeni Plushenko, Emanuel Sandhu, Min Zhang (2006, short program)
WORLDS: Stéphane Lambiel, Min Zhang (2005, Qualifying Group B)
EUROPEANS: Brian Joubert, Stéphane Lambiel (2005, short program)

FOUR CONTINENTS: Chengjiang Li, Daisuke Takahashi, Min Zhang (2005, short program)

Quad toe-loop (women)

OLYMPICS: Kamila Valieva[122] (2022, team even free skate)
EUROPEANS: Alexandra Trusova (2020, free skate)

---

[122] "IOC: No medal ceremony for team event, or women's singles if Valieva is top three", NBC Olympics, February 14, 2022 (updated February 15, 2022)

The Loop

The loop jump is an edge jump that takes off and lands on the back outside edge of the same foot.

The man credited with inventing the loop was Werner Rittberger of Germany, who won a trio of silver medals at the World Championships from 1910 to 1912, as well as four medals at the European Championships - both before and after The Great War.[123]

German skating historian Dr. Matthias Hampe explained, "Werner Rittberger developed the legend that in 1909, he skated dreamily in the Berliner Eispalast on Lutherstraße to the music "Wie einst im Mai" by Walter Kollo and reacted spontaneously to a change in rhythm or a drumbeat in the music with his loop jump. In 1961 he explained in the specialist publication 'Deutscher Eissport': "Following the music, I circled, did pirouettes and jumps as my

---

[123] "Faszination Eissport: 100 Jahre Eissport", Heinz Maegerlein, 1986

muscles suggested. Suddenly I realized what kind of jump I was actually doing, which I had unconsciously jumped after listening to the music.' However, his grandson Michael Rittberger assumed that the jump was developed during training and rated the anecdote as a clever advertising strategy."[124]

The jump, believed to have been performed for the first time internationally at the 1910 World Championships in Davos, soon became known in Europe as 'the Rittberger'. In North America, it was known in the 1920s and 1930s as 'the back-loop jump'[125].

In the roaring twenties, a small handful of skaters began experimenting with double jumps. These attempts would hardly meet the scrutiny of today's technical panels. If you stood up, you landed a jump - as far as most judges were concerned in those early days. One of the first skaters to be credited with landing the double loop in competition was Canada's Montgomery 'Bud' Wilson at the

---

[124] Interview with Dr. Matthias Hampe, January 10, 2023; "Werner Rittberger in der 'Hall of Fame' des Eiskunstlaufs", Dr. Matthias Hampe, "Pirouette" magazine, May-June 2017

[125] "Some Jumps at a Glance", Mrs. Lenox Napier, "Skating" magazine, March 1936

1929 North American Championships in Boston.[126] He included the jump in his medal-winning program at the 1932 Winter Olympic Games in Lake Placid.[127]

By the start of World War II, the double loop was a fairly common element in men's free skating programs. Skaters like Felix Kaspar[128], Robin Lee[129], Ralph McCreath[130], Lloyd 'Skippy' Baxter[131], William Grimditch Jr.[132] and Wally Sahlin[133] all had the jump in their arsenal. Rather than go for two rotations, 1939 European and World Champion Graham Sharp's trademark move was a series of three to five single loop jumps in a row, timed to his music and performed to great

---

126 "Impressions: North American Championships", Norman V.S. Gregory, "Skating" magazine, May 1929
127 "Die Genese des Eiskunstlaufens als Prozess der Versportung und struktureller Veränderungen im Wettkampfsystem sowie der Leistungsentwicklung", Dr. Matthias Hampe, Humanwissenschaftlichen Fakultät der Universität Potsdam, 2010
128 "Summer Skating in London", M. Bernard Fox, "Skating" magazine, December 1935
129 "Robin Lee: A Champion Revisited", Durant Imboden, "Skating" magazine, January 1991
130 "The Canadian Championships", Joan Parkins, "Skating" magazine, March 1940
131 "Rockers and Counters", "Skating" magazine, January 1938
132 "Meet The Champions", "Skating" magazine, March 1941
133 "Meet The Champions", Benjamin T. Wright, "Skating" magazine, April 1942

effect.[134]

One of the first accounts of a woman performing a double loop was Barbara Ann Scott, at a Red Cross Carnival and Masquerade at the first Canadian summer skating school in Kitchener in 1940[135]. She was only twelve years old at the time. By 1948, women were attempting double loops left, right and center. Barbara Ann Scott, Ája Zanová, and Jeannette Altwegg all tried the jump in their Olympic free skating programs that year. America's Gretchen Merrill even attempted two.[136] Barbara Ann Scott continued performing the jump well into her professional career. In 1965, she reminisced, "I always liked to put in a double loop just for my own satisfaction, and somewhere up in the audience maybe one little bit of clapping would tell me there was a skater in the crowd. Of course, today a double loop doesn't mean anything; they all do triple loops."[137]

---

134 "Reviewing the British Championships", Dennis L. Bird (under pseudonym John Noel), "Skating World" magazine, February 1948

135 "Much Skating -- No War, at Kitchener", Dr. A.E. Broome and Madge Austin, "Skating" magazine, October 1940

136 "Olympic Day", Nigel Brown, "Skating World" magazine, March 1948; "The Olympics - 1948", Theresa Weld Blanchard, "Skating" magazine, April 1948

137 "Reflections of a Champion", Martha H. Roynon, "Skating" magazine, November 1965

The first skater to land the triple loop was of course Dick Button, at the 1952 Winter Olympics and World Championships. A master of the edge jump, Button had already made history as the first skater to land three double loops in succession and a double Axel/double loop combination[138] before he pulled off the triple. He was coached by Gustave Lussi, a pioneering technical coach who along with Sheldon Galbraith and Edi Scholdan was a pioneer of the introduction of the back spin air position in jumps. [139] In Button's 1955 book, he wrote poetically about how the jump seemed to come to him in slow motion in the freezing cold and wind at the Oslo Olympics. The momentous occasion of the first triple jump achieved in Olympic competition was not lost on the Norwegian audience, who erupted in a thundering applause.[140]

It didn't take long at all for the triple loop to become the benchmark in men's figure

---

[138] "Die Genese des Eiskunstlaufens als Prozess der Versportung und struktureller Veränderungen im Wettkampfsystem sowie der Leistungsentwicklung", Dr. Matthias Hampe, Humanwissenschaftlichen Fakultät der Universität Potsdam, 2010
[139] Interview with Donald Jackson, The Manleywoman SkateCast, November 28, 2013
[140] "Dick Button on Skates", Dick Button, 1955

skating. David Jenkins landed the jump at the Midwestern Championships at the Broadmoor in Colorado Springs in 1953[141] as well as at the 1954 World Championships, also held in Oslo.[142] By the early 1960s, a handful of the world's best skaters were attempting it in their programs, including Alain Calmat[143], Donald McPherson[144] and Karol Divín[145].

There has been some debate over the years as to who the first woman to land the triple loop was. One contemporary German source credits Austria's Helli Sengstschmid as being the first, in 1963[146], but this was not reported at the time. East Germany's Gaby Seyfert was landing the triple loop in practice as early as 1966.[147] She stood up on the jump at the 1968

---

141 "Midwesterns", Mrs. Steve Kaufman, "Skating" magazine, April 1953
142 "The Championships of the World", William O. Hickok ICV, Mrs. William Rhein, Dorothy Ogelsby and Theodore G. Patterson, "Skating" magazine, April 1954
143 "1963 French Championships", Jane Vaughn Sullivan, "Skating" magazine, March 1963
144 "The 1963 North American Championships", Capilano Winter Club members, "Skating" magazine, April 1963
145 "Olympic Drama", Dennis L. Bird (under pseudonym John Noel), "Skating" magazine, April 1964
146 "Eislaufen: Eiskunstlauf, Inline-Kunstlauf, Eistanz, Synchronlaufen, Eischnellauf, Eishockey, Spiele auf dem Eis", Siegmar-Walter Breckle, 2019
147 "Skating on TV", Dennis L. Bird (writing under the pseudonym John Noel), "Skating World" magazine, March 1966

European Championships in Västerås but was short on rotation[148]. She has still been credited as the first to successfully land it in competition.[149] The following year, Czechoslovakia's Hana Mašková took a tumble on a triple loop attempt at the European Championships in Garmisch-Partenkirchen.[150]

Fourteen-year-old Priscilla Hill landed the triple loop at the 1975 Prague Skate and 1976 Eastern Championships[151], and as far as the USFSA was concerned, she was the first to land it successfully. In 1978, an article in "Skating" magazine claimed that only eight women had successfully landed the jump in competition - Washington state's Staci Loop and Jill Sawyer, Utah's Suzie Brasher, Georgia's Jackie Farrell, Switzerland's Denise Biellmann, West Germany's Dagmar Lurz and the Soviet Union's Elena Vodorezova.[152] The author neglected to mention Gaby Seyfert's attempt a

---

148 Video footage
149 "Olympic champions lead 2019 World Hall of Fame", World Figure Skating Museum & Hall of Fame, 2019
150 "1969 European Championships", Dennis L. Bird, "Skating" magazine, April 1969; Video footage
151 "Easterns: Broadway Performance", Astrid Hagenguth, "Skating" magazine, February 1976
152 "Silver Screen Skating", Debbie Stoery, "Skating" magazine, November 1978

decade prior.

In 1991, Kurt Browning landed a triple Salchow/triple loop combination at the World Championships in Munich, making history as the first skater to land a triple loop as the second jump in any combination at an ISU Championships.[153] Five years later, France's Éric Millot made history as the first skater to land a triple loop/triple loop combination in international competition[154]. Tara Lipinski became the first skater to land the triple loop/triple loop on Olympic ice in Nagano in 1998.[155]

The next mountain to climb was the quad loop... and the first skater to land it in competition was Japan's Yuzuru Hanyu, in the short program at the Autumn Classic International in Montreal in 2016.[156]

---

153 "Die Genese des Eiskunstlaufens als Prozess der Versportung und struktureller Veränderungen im Wettkampfsystem sowie der Leistungsentwicklung", Dr. Matthias Hampe, Humanwissenschaftlichen Fakultät der Universität Potsdam, 2010
154 "Urmanov tops Elvis; Edmonton 'shootout' predicted by coach; Champions Series Final", Cam Cole, "The Edmonton Journal", February 25, 1996
155 "It's Tara's world: Lipinski defies tradition to overcome Kwan in showdown", Steve Milton, "Calgary Herald", February 21, 1998
156 "Yuzuru Hanyu (JPN) performs first clean quad loop in competition", International Skating Union, October 2, 2016

TECHNICAL FIRSTS UNDER THE IJS SYSTEM

Only jumps receiving a 0 or positive GOE were considered when compiling this data.

Triple loop (men)

OLYMPICS: Chengjiang Li, Shawn Sawyer (2006, short program)
WORLDS: Kristoffer Berntsson, Jeffrey Buttle, Samuel Contesti, Timothy Goebel, Brian Joubert, Stéphane Lambiel, Kevin van der Perren, Tomáš Verner (2005, Qualifying Group B)
EUROPEANS: Kristoffer Berntsson, Andrei Griazev, John Hamer, Brian Joubert, Stéphane Lambiel, Martin Liebers, Stefan Lindemann, Jamal Othman, Viktor Pfeifer, Kevin van der Perren (2005, free skate)
FOUR CONTINENTS: Chengjiang Li (2005, short program)

Triple loop (women)

OLYMPICS: Carolina Kostner, Yan Liu (2006, short program)
WORLDS: Miki Ando, Idora Hegel, Júlia Sebestyén, Yelena Sokolova (2005, Qualifying Round B)
EUROPEANS: Kiira Korpi, Roxana Luca (2005, short program)
FOUR CONTINENTS: Lesley Hawker, Jennifer Kirk, Yan Liu, Yoshie Onda (2005, free skate)

Quad loop (men)

OLYMPICS: Yuma Kagiyama (2022, team event free skate)
WORLDS: Yuzuru Hanyu (2017, short program)
EUROPEANS: Daniel Grassl (2019, short program)
FOUR CONTINENTS: Yuzuru Hanyu (2017, short program)

EULER ALERT

The ISU opted to officially name the half loop the Euler during the 2018/2019 season, but the name is far from new. The terms Euler and half-loop were used interchangeably in the CFSA's Rulebook as early as the 1980s. The jump is presumably named after Austrian brothers Karl and Gustav Euler, who won the same-sex pairs event at the 1900 European Championships in Berlin. Same-sex pairs skating was contested at both the World and European Championships at the turn of the century. The Euler Brothers were both exceptional jumpers who performed one-and-a-half turn rotation jumps in one of their performances together at the Training Eis-Klub in Vienna at the turn of the century.

The Flip

Taking off from a left back inside edge and landing on a right back outside edge, the flip jump is traditionally considered the second most difficult toe-assisted jump. Unlike the Axel and Lutz, which you will read about later, the flip was not named after its inventor. Its history is perhaps the most murky of any of skating's jumps.

Montgomery 'Bud' Wilson developed the jump with coach Gustave Lussi in Canada. Mr. Lussi stated that when Evelyn Chandler came up to Canada to perform, she saw the jump performed and took it down to the States.[157]

In America, the jump became known as a Mapes - after Evelyn Chandler's husband Bruce Mapes, who invented the toe-loop. The reason why the Mapes name caught on in America, stated Walter Arian in 1943, was because Evelyn Chandler Mapes performed the jump so frequently in her free skating

---

[157] "Biographical Sketch of Gustave Lussi", Cecily Morrow

performances.[158] Interestingly, in roller skating today a toe-loop jump - not a flip - is known as a Mapes.[159]

It took several years for the term 'flip' to stick. In the thirties in Canada, the jump was often referred to as the Wilson, after Montgomery Wilson.[160] The names toe-Salchow[161] and toe-point Salchow[162] were also used for the jump in the 1930s and 1940s.

Montgomery Wilson was one of the first skaters to attempt a double and he was of the belief that his pupil, Janette Ahrens, was the first woman to accomplish a double successfully.[163]

The jump had achieved widespread popularity by the World War II era. Guy Owen performed it, along with the 'flip-and-a-

---

158 "Jumps: Description and History", "Skating" magazine, December 1943
159 "The Complete Book of Roller Skating", Ann-Victoria Phillips, 1979
160 "Jumps: Description and History", "Skating" magazine, December 1943
161 "Revision of N.S.A. Figure Skating Tests in the International Style", "Skating World" magazine, November 1948
162 "Double Flip Jump", Montgomery Wilson, "Skating" magazine, October 1940
163 Ibid

half variation, which his then-wife Maribel considered one of his best jumps.[164] Pairs like Rosemarie Stewart and Bob Dench were landing side-by-side flips during the War.[165]

As a young man, Dick Button was dubbed the President of the 'Double Flip Club' after having a terrible fall on the jump during a practice session at Lake Placid.[166] The split flip and double flip later became two of Dick's finer jumps. He was the first skater to perform the jump in an ISU Championship, at the 1947 European Championships in Davos.[167]

By the early 1950s, a small group of women, including Germany's Gundi Busch[168], Czechoslovakia's Dagmar Lerchová[169], the UK's

---

164 "Maribel Y. Vinson's Advanced Figure Skating", Maribel Vinson Owen, 1940
165 "Pair Skating and Dancing on Ice", Rosemarie Stewart and Bob Dench, 1943
166 "Dick Button on Skates", Dick Button, 1955
167 "Die Genese des Eiskunstlaufens als Prozess der Versportung und struktureller Veränderungen im Wettkampfsystem sowie der Leistungsentwicklung", Dr. Matthias Hampe, Humanwissenschaftlichen Fakultät der Universität Potsdam, 2010
168 "European Championships", Captain T.D. Richardson, "Skating World" magazine, March 1954
169 "Championships of Czechoslovakia", "Skating World" magazine, February 1950

Pat Devries[170] and Americans Carol Heiss[171] and Yvonne Sherman[172] had the jump in their repertoires.

Donald Jackson began jazzing things up and performing a unique variation of the double flip with his hands on his hips[173].

Triple flip chatter started in the late 1950s, when David Jenkins attempted the jump in his free skating performance at the World Championships, unfortunately erring in the landing.[174]. In his 2011 interview with Allison Manley for The Manleywoman SkateCast[175], David admitted to having "pretty much accomplished" the triple flip before attending medical school but did not discuss attempting it in Paris.

A report on the 1961 North American

---

170 "British Olympic Trials", "Skating World" magazine, January 1952
171 "The United States Championships", Sandy Thomas, "Skating" magazine, May 1953
172 "American Scene", "Skating World" magazine, November 1949
173 "You're An Old Softie", Betty Campbell, "Skating" magazine, June 1972
174 Handwritten notes by Dennis L. Bird; "World's Figure Skating Championships", Captain T.D. Richardson, "Skating World" magazine, March 1958; Interview with Frazer Ormondroyd, January 4, 2023
175 Interview with David Jenkins, Allison Manley, The Manleywoman SkateCast, April 7, 2011

Championships that appeared in "Skating" magazine claimed Donald Jackson landed the triple flip[176], but Jackson has confirmed that this was incorrect, as the only two triples he ever did in competition were the Salchow and Lutz.[177] In a report in "Winter Sports" magazine, Howard Bass claimed that Austria's Wolfgang Schwarz landed the flip in his free skate at the 1967 European Championships[178], but this was not a jump that was included in Schwarz's other programs.[179] It is likely that those reviewing these events misidentified the jumps with another with a three turn entry - the Salchow.

America's John 'Misha' Petkevich planned the triple flip for his free skate at the 1968 U.S. Championships but pulled the jump from his program after pulling a muscle in his leg. Interestingly, Petkevich created a jump he called the Bourkey, after his coach Arthur Bourke.[180] A variation of the flip with a side

---

176 "The North American Championships", Suzanne Davis King, "Skating" magazine, April 1961
177 Interview with Donald Jackson, January 1, 2023
178 "Europe's Exciting Prelude To Vienna", Howard Bass, "Winter Sports" magazine, March 1967
179 Video footage
180 "Bold Bourkey For John Misha", Bob Ottum, "Sports Illustrated" magazine, January 29, 1968

stag position in the air, the jump was based on an airborne picture of ballet dancer Rudolf Nureyev.[181]

In the 1970s – a decade when artistically gifted skaters like Toller Cranston and John Curry reigned supreme - several men worked to push the envelope technically by expanding their repertoire of triple jumps beyond the toe-loop and Salchow. Soviet skater Yuri Ovchinnikov mastered four (the toe-loop, Salchow, loop and flip) and Terry Kubicka mastered five (the toe-loop, Salchow, loop, flip and Lutz).[182] Fumio Igarashi, Minoru Sano, Igor Bobrin, David Santee and Vern Taylor also landed the triple flip in competition during the 'disco decade'. Mitsuru Matsumura was certainly capable of the jump as well.[183] American skater Mark Cockerell included a unique half-flip/triple flip combination in his free skate in 1978.[184]

But who was the very first skater to land it in competition? Richard Ewell III landed the

---

[181] Interview with John 'Misha' Petkevich, Allison Manley, The Manleywoman SkateCast, December 13, 2013
[182] Video footage
[183] Ibid
[184] "Pacific Coasts", "Skating" magazine, March 1978

jump in his free skate at the 1972 U.S. Championships in Long Beach, California - a first at the U.S. Championships.[185] At the time, he was not recognized for his achievement in print. The first account in "Skating" magazine of the jump being performed in competition was by Jimmy Demogines, at the 1974 Eastern Great Lakes Championships in Troy, Ohio.[186] It has been claimed that Czechoslovakian skater Zdeněk Pazdírek landed a triple flip at the 1974 World Championships, but video footage has not been readily available for verification.[187]

Where there were so many skaters in different countries working on the triple flip around the same time, the first skater to perform the triple flip is still a hot topic of debate.

In the early years of the singles short program, there were four groups of required elements. Each year, the ISU would do a draw

---

185 Interview with Richard Ewell, June 2021
186 "Eastern Great Lakes", Karla Boyles, "Skating" magazine, February 1974"
187 "Die Genese des Eiskunstlaufens als Prozess der Versportung und struktureller Veränderungen im Wettkampfsystem sowie der Leistungsentwicklung", Dr. Matthias Hampe, Humanwissenschaftlichen Fakultät der Universität Potsdam, 2010

to select which group would be skated, similar to the draws for school figures.[188] Before the 1978/1979 season, 'Group 1' was selected. Little did the officials, coaches and skaters know that the required "two jump combination, consisting of a double flip together with another double jump or triple jump" would prove to be somewhat of a disaster.[189] Skaters again struggled with the flip combination[190] when 'Group 1' was chosen for the 1981/1982 season.[191] Brian Pockar 'beat the system' in the short program at the 1979 World Championships, making history with an extremely rare one-foot triple Salchow/double flip combination.[192]

By the late 1980s, when Brian Boitano and Brian Orser battled it out in the Battle Of The Brian's at the Calgary Olympics, the triple flip was considered a 'must have' jump. It was so close between Boitano and Orser in 1988 that some argued it was Orser's faulty landing on

---

188 Canadian Figure Skating Association Rulebook, 1980
189 "Landing It: My Life On and Off the Ice", Scott Hamilton and Lorenzo Benet, 1999
190 "Orser: A Skater's Life", Brian Orser and Steve Milton, 1988
191 "Official Notes - Senior Men & Ladies Short Program Elements", "Skating" magazine, October 1981
192 "U.S. skaters take pairs title", "The Globe and Mail", March 15, 1979

the flip that cost him the gold.¹⁹³

Who was the first woman to land the triple flip? A report in "Skating" magazine suggested that Linda Fratianne may have performed the jump in her free skate at the 1978 Pacific Coast Championships in Burbank, California.¹⁹⁴ A young East German skater, Karin Miegel, also landed the jump around this time.¹⁹⁵

As for the first woman to land the jump in international competition, a very strong candidate is Lynn Smith of the St. Moritz Ice Skating Club in California. Unbelievable as it may sound, Smith landed a triple flip, triple loop and two triple Lutzes (one in combination with a double toe-loop)¹⁹⁶ on her way to winning the Grand Prix International de France in St. Gervais in August of 1978.¹⁹⁷ Smith wasn't only a prodigal free skater – she won the figures in the senior women's event

---

193 "Oh Canada; $25-million Best Ever program has yet to produce gold medal", Julian Beltrame, "The Ottawa Citizen", February 22, 1988
194 "Pacific Coasts", "Skating" magazine, March 1978
195 WDR - Sport Inside, "Staatsdoping - Menschenversuche im DDR-Sport"
196 Interview with Frazer Ormondroyd, January 4, 2023; Video footage
197 "Ice Abroad", "Skating"' magazine, October 1979

over World Champion Linda Fratianne at the 1979 U.S. Championships in Cincinnati, Ohio.[198]

The ISU has credited East Germany's Katarina Witt and West Germany's Manuela Ruben as being the first women to land a triple flip in an ISU Championship, at the 1981 European Championships in Innsbruck.[199] However, Witt doubled her attempt at that event. German skating historian Dr. Matthias Hampe noted that at the 1981 World Championships, Witt was the first to attempt the jump at the World Championships. She landed the jump on two feet and her teammate Carola Paul successfully performed a triple flip in competition the same year.[200]

Not long after, Midori Ito[201], Claudia

---

198 "Nationals: A Bird's-Eye View", Mary-Lucile Ager, "Skating" magazine, April 1979
199 "ISU Figure Skating Media Guide 2022/2023", International Skating Union
200 "Die Genese des Eiskunstlaufens als Prozess der Versportung und struktureller Veränderungen im Wettkampfsystem sowie der Leistungsentwicklung", Dr. Matthias Hampe, Humanwissenschaftlichen Fakultät der Universität Potsdam, 2010
201 "Skate Canada '84 Victoria", Carole Stafford, "Skating" magazine, January 1985

Leistner[202], Kay Thomson[203], Tiffany Chin[204] and Jill Trenary[205] added the difficult jump to their repertoires. Interestingly, Katarina Witt didn't include the jump in either of her Olympic gold medal-winning performances.[206]

The first Olympic Gold Medallist in women's figure skating to land the triple flip in her winning performance was Kristi Yamaguchi[207], who was already doing the jump in competition as a junior as early as 1985.[208] As a teenager, Yamaguchi also made history by landing the first side-by-side triple flips with partner Rudy Galindo.[209]

At the 2010 World Championships in Torino, Italy, Daisuke Takahashi daringly attempted a quad flip in his free skate.[210] He under-rotated the jump but made history as the first

---

202 "Skate" Yearbook ("Ice & Roller Skate" magazine), 1986
203 "Canadians '83 - The Women - Thomson Dominates", Beverley Smith, "The Canadian Skater" magazine, February/March 1983
204 "Skate" Yearbook ("Ice & Roller Skate" magazine), 1986
205 Video footage
206 Ibid
207 Ibid
208 "Report: Central Pacific", Cherie Shellack, "Skating" magazine, February 1986
209 "'86 Skate America", "Skating" magazine, December 1986
210 Video footage

Japanese man ever to win a World title.[211] Six years later, Shoma Uno became the first skater to land a ratified quad flip at the 2016 KOSÉ Team Challenge Cup in Spokane, Washington.[212] In 2018, Nathan Chen became the first skater to land the quad flip at the Olympic Games.[213] Alexandra Trusova became the first woman to land the jump at the 2019 Grand Prix Final.[214]

TECHNICAL FIRSTS UNDER THE IJS SYSTEM

Only jumps receiving a 0 or positive GOE were considered when compiling this data.

Triple flip (men)

OLYMPICS: Jeffrey Buttle, Frédéric Dambier, Brian Joubert, Anton Kovalevski, Stefan Lindemann, Viktor Pfeifer, Shawn Sawyer, Matt Savoie, Zoltán Tóth, Tomáš Verner, Johnny Weir, Trifun Živanović (2006, short program)

---

211 "Takahashi is first Japanese man to win", Associated Press/ESPN, March 25, 2010
212 "Quad-o-mania: An overview of the quad jumps' history", International Skating Union, February 2022
213 "All of the figure skating firsts from PyeongChang 2018", Rachel Lutz, NBC Olympics, February 24, 2018
214 "ISU Figure Skating Media Guide 2022/2023", International Skating Union

WORLDS: Jeffrey Buttle, Gheorghe Chiper, Samuel Contesti, Frédéric Dambier, Brian Joubert, Maciej Kuś, Evan Lysacek, Daisuke Takahashi, Trifun Živanović, Min Zhang (2005, Qualifying Group B)
EUROPEANS: Paolo Bacchini, Gheorghe Chiper, John Hamer, Brian Joubert, Maciej Kuś, Andrei Lezin, Martin Liebers, Viktor Pfeifer, Lukáš Rakowski, Roman Serov (2005, short program)
FOUR CONTINENTS: Ben Ferreira, Shawn Sawyer, Matt Savoie (2005, short program)

Triple flip (women)

OLYMPICS: Miki Ando, Sasha Cohen, Galina Efremenko, Emily Hughes, Kiira Korpi, Mira Leung, Sarah Meier, Kimmie Meissner, Júlia Sebestyén, Irina Slutskaya, Fumie Suguri (2006, short program)
WORLDS: Joanne Carter, Sasha Cohen, Annette Dytrt, Idora Hegel, Lina Johansson, Yan Liu, Susanna Pöykiö, Júlia Sebestyén (2005, Qualifying Group B)
EUROPEANS: Joanne Carter, Jennifer Kirk, Beatrisa Liang, Yoshie Onda, Fumie Suguri (2005, short program)
FOUR CONTINENTS:

Quad flip (men)

OLYMPICS: Shoma Uno (2018, short program)
WORLDS: Nathan Chen, Shoma Uno (2017, short program)
EUROPEANS: Daniel Grassl (2020, free skate)
FOUR CONTINENTS: Nathan Chen (2017, short program)

Quad flip (women)

OLYMPICS: Anna Shcherbakova (2022, free skate)
WORLDS: -*
EUROPEANS: Anna Shcherbakova, Alexandra Trusova (2022, free skate)

*Anna Shcherbakova and Alexandra Trusova both attempted quad flips at the 2021 World Championships. Anna's attempt was judged as landing on a quarter turn and she received a negative GOE. Alexandra's attempt received a positive GOE but was called for an unclear take-off edge.

FLIPPING OUT OVER FLIP FACTS

For many years, the flip jump was known as the 'toe Salchow' in Canada. The toe-loop was known as the 'cherry flip'.

Three popular variations of the flip jump are the half-flip (half a rotation from RBI - LFI/RFO), split flip (one rotation from RBI-LBO with a brief split position/delay in mid-air) and one-and-a-half-flip (one-and-a-half rotations from RBI-RFO).

The Lutz

The most difficult of the toe-assisted jumps because of its counter-rotation, the Lutz takes off from a back outside edge, landing on the back outside edge of the other foot.

The invention of the Lutz has been credited to an unheralded Austrian skater named Alois Lutz. For many years, alternating accounts citing a grand total of (wait for it!) zero primary sources, alternately traced his grand performance of the Lutz to the Edwardian era[215], 1913[216] and 1918[217] - as well as long after his death, in the 1930s[218] and 1940s[219]. It has been said he died of pneumonia[220] or the Spanish flu[221] in his early twenties, but again, no primary sources there either. One book

---

215 "Now You Know Big Book of Sports", Doug Lennox, 2009
216 "The jumps, spins and turns of figure skating", Olympics.com, October 17, 2018
217 "Ice Skating: From Axels to Zambonis", Dan Gutman, 1995
218 "Winter Games Made Simple: A Guide for Spectators & Television Viewers", Dan Bartges, 1993
219 "World of Sports Science", K. Lee Lerner and Brenda Wilmoth Lerner, 2007
220 "100 years of Lutz jump", Olga Fluegge, World Figure Skating, November 29, 2013
221 Post on rec.sport.skating.ice.figure newsgroup, January 6, 2001

claimed that he was a European Champion.[222] Others claimed his name was Alfred[223] or Tomas Lutz[224]. To be blunt, the lack of information about this little-known, young skater and the origins of his invention has inspired many writers over the decades to repeat unsourced information or in most cases, just plain make stuff up. Dr. Matthias Hampe was the first to research Alois Lutz's story in depth, publishing many interesting facts about his life in "The Journal of The Figure Skating Historical Society", a short-lived periodical that was published in the mid-1990s.[225] Dr. Hampe uncovered a great deal more information when he penned another extensively researched article on Lutz for "Pirouette" magazine in 2022. It was learned that he was born in poor circumstances and worked as an apprentice to a mechanic after attending school. Three-time European Champion Eduard Engelmann Jr. recognized his talent and without his support, he would

---

222 "World of Sports Science", K. Lee Lerner and Brenda Wilmoth Lerner, 2007
223 "Les étoiles du patinage: 16 affiches en couleurs des plus grandes étoiles du patinage!", Allison Gertridge, 1994
224 "The Encyclopedia of Figure Skating", John Williams Malone, 1998
225 "Alois Lutz", Matthias Hampe, "The Journal of the Figure Skating Historical Society", Spring 1995

not have been able to afford to skate. He competed in several domestic competitions in Vienna beginning in 1912[226] and was praised for his speed, clever footwork, "unusual inventiveness... in his original jumps" at a club competition in Vienna in 1913.[227] He played on bandy and Eisball (football on ice) teams and registered in speed skating competitions in Vienna during The Great War, last competing in a figure skating competition in 1917. He was drafted into military service that year, returning with pulmonary tuberculosis and dying on February 15, 1918, at the age of nineteen.[228]

The survival and attribution of Lutz's jump can likely be traced to his connection with Eduard Engelmann Jr. and the fact that he trained in Vienna, which was very much an important epicenter of figure skating in the early twentieth century.

Reports of other skaters doing the Lutz jump started cropping up in the roaring twenties.

---

226 "Neuentdeckungen über Alois Lutz", Dr. Matthias Hampe, "Pirouette" magazine, July/August 2022
227 Interview with Dr. Matthias Hampe, January 10, 2023
228 "Neuentdeckungen über Alois Lutz", Dr. Matthias Hampe, "Pirouette" magazine, July/August 2022

One of the first written records of the Lutz jump was Dr. Otto Preißecker's inclusion of it in his program at the 1928 Austrian Championships, though Dr. Hampe noted that it is likely that other top Austrian skaters like Karl Schäfer "had already performed this jump before, albeit undocumented by the press."[229] Captain T.D. Richardson recalled, "There is a popular jump called the Lutz which I first saw performed by that grand skater Paul Kreckow at the Palazzo del Ghiaccio in Milan in the early 20's. It is a joyous affair and should be tackled, once its technique is understood, with complete abandon."[230] Though the Lutz jump made it out of Austria in the 1920s, it was not commonplace in North America until the 1930s.[231]

Though Barbara Ann Scott has been credited as the first skater to perform a double Lutz jump in competition, in the junior women's event at the 1942 Canadian Championships in Winnipeg, Manitoba[232], it has been

---
229 "Neuentdeckungen über Alois Lutz", Dr. Matthias Hampe, "Pirouette" magazine, July/August 2022
230 "Skating with T.D. Richardson", Captain T.D. Richardson, 1952
231 "Maribel Y. Vinson's Advanced Figure Skating", Maribel Vinson Owen, 1940
232 "Canadian figure skating legend Barbara Ann Scott dies", The

recorded that Skippy Baxter was doing the jump in exhibitions as early as 1941.[233] The first skater to perform a double Lutz in an ISU Championship was Dick Button, at the 1947 European Championships in Davos.[234]

By the time the 1952 Winter Olympic Games in Oslo rolled around, a handful of elite skaters had the double Lutz in their repertoire, including Ája Zanová, Jacqueline du Bief, Michael Carrington[235], Carlo Fassi[236] and Austin Holt[237]. Zanová has been credited as the first woman to land a double Lutz at the World Championships in 1949.[238] An account of the competition published in "Skating World" magazine praised Zanova's "many difficult jumps" but failed to mention a double Lutz specifically. It did, however, praise

---

Canadian Press/CBC, September 30, 2012
233 "Champ Fancy Skaters To Entertain Fans", "Daily News", January 17, 1941
234 "Die Genese des Eiskunstlaufens als Prozess der Versportung und struktureller Veränderungen im Wettkampfsystem sowie der Leistungsentwicklung", Dr. Matthias Hampe, Humanwissenschaftlichen Fakultät der Universität Potsdam, 2010
235 "British Figure Skating Championships", Clare Leslie, "Skating World" magazine, January 1950
236 "The European Figure Skating Championships", "Skating World" magazine, March 1951
237 "1950 Championships of the World", Kenneth D. McRae, "Skating" magazine, May 1950
238 "Aja Zanova, Top Czech Skater Who Defected to West, Dies at 84", Margalit Fox, The New York Times, August 1, 2015

Jacqueline du Bief's "very high double Lutz."[239]

One of the most remarkable achievements in figure skating history was the first triple Lutz. In the case of almost every single 'first' discussed in this book, multiple skaters have been working on the same jump around the same time. That simply wasn't the case when Donald Jackson took an unprecedented risk and achieved a historic first at the 1962 World Championships in Prague, Czechoslovakia. Though a gifted jumper who regularly included triple Salchows in his free skating program[240], Jackson began working on the jump in practice with Pierre Brunet until a hard fall on the jump resulted in a severe ankle sprain, which resulted in him having to wear an ankle foot cast for several weeks.[241] Work on the triple Lutz resumed when he started working with Sheldon Galbraith. He worked on the triple Lutz with his feet side by side and not in a back spin position because he was training that way before he came to Galbraith. He respected Mr.

---

[239] "The World's Figure Skating Championships", Dennis L. Bird (writing under the pseudonym John Noel), "Skating World" magazine, March 1949
[240] Video footage
[241] "Donald Jackson: King Of Blades", George Gross, 1977

Galbraith for letting him continue in his technique.[242] He first attempted the jump in competition at the 1962 Canadian Championships, two-footing the landing. He had only landed a handful of clean triple Lutzes in practice.

When Donald Jackson was getting ready to take the ice for his free skate at the 1962 World Championships, a judge said to Sheldon Galbraith, "Why are you letting that young man do that?", to which he replied, "He wants to do it, let him do it, he's worked hard at it."[243] The triple Lutz that Jackson landed in his performance wasn't duplicated in competition for over a decade, underscoring just how ahead of its time it truly was. It was truly akin to a train being invented before the wheel.

John 'Misha' Petkevich attempted a triple Lutz at the 1969 North American Championships in Oakland but took an unfortunate tumble.[244] The same fate befell Japan's Minoru

---
242 Interview with Donald Jackson, January 7, 2023
243 Interview with Donald Jackson, Allison Manley, The Manleywoman SkateCast, November 18, 2013
244 "1969 North American Championships: U.S. and Canadian skaters meet in friendly rivalry", Joy Janes, "Skating" magazine, April 1969

Sano, who fell on an attempt at the 1973 World Championships in Bratislava. British skater Haig Oundjian was reportedly landing the jump in practice in the early 1970s.[245]

In the autumn of 1972, Terry Kubicka landed triple Lutzes in both Regional and Sectional competitions but fell in his attempt to make history as the first man to land the jump at the U.S. Championships in 1973.[246] He achieved his dream in 1974, landing the first triple Lutzes at the U.S. Championships - one in combination with a double toe-loop in the short program and a solo triple Lutz in the free skate.[247]

Vern Taylor had the unusual distinction of landing the first two triple Lutzes at the Canadian Championships. He landed the first in 1973, when he won the Canadian novice men's title, and the second in 1976[248], when he won the junior title.[249] Like Donald Jackson,

---

245 Interview with Frazer Ormondroyd, January 4, 2023; Video footage
246 "Nationals '73", Sal Zanca, "Skating" magazine, April 1973
247 "Nationals", Sal Zanca, "Skating" magazine, April 1974
248 "Canadians", Betty Ann Bagley, March 1976
249 Results of the 1973 and 1976 Canadian Championships, "The Almanac of Canadian Figure Skating", Ryan Stevens

Taylor was coached by Sheldon Galbraith.[250]

Jan Hoffmann overrotated an attempt at the triple Lutz in his winning program at the 1974 European Championships[251] but landed the jump at the World Championships that year in Munich.[252] However, he wasn't the second man to land the triple Lutz at the World Championships. He was beaten to the punch by László Vajda, who landed the jump in the short program at the same event.[253]

Two years later at the World Championships in Gothenburg, Glyn Jones made history as the first British skater to land a triple Lutz at the World Championships and Japan's Minoru Sano landed a triple Lutz in combination with a double toe-loop.[254] In her "BBC Book of Skating", Sandra Stevenson remarked, "Although Robin Cousins did triple Lutzes in practice and used them to disconcert Vladimir Kovalev, USSR, he did not find it

---

250 "Master Coach Sheldon Galbraith Leaves Lasting Legacy", Skate Canada, April 30, 2015
251 "Europeans", "Skating" magazine, April 1974
252 "An Overview of Worlds", Frank Nowosad, "Skating" magazine, May 1974
253 Interview with Frazer Ormondroyd, January 4, 2023; Video footage
254 "Dalby's Worldly Diary", Peter Dalby, "Skating" magazine, May 1976

necessary to include this jump in his competitive routines. Commentating for BBC during the 1983 World Championships, Cousins expressed his amazement that more than half the men in that event successfully presented the triple Lutz in combination with a double toe-loop in the short programme division. It was yet another mark of skating's technical progress."[255]

Tacoma, Washington teenager Jill Sawyer, a student of Kathy Casey[256], was one of the first women to have a triple Lutz in her bag of tricks.[257] She 'only' landed a triple Salchow and toe-loop[258] when she won the first official ISU World Junior Championships in Megéve, France in March of 1978.

The first woman to land a triple Lutz in international competition was Switzerland's Denise Biellmann, at the 1978 European Championships in Strasbourg, France.[259] The next two women to achieve success with the

---

255 "The BBC Book of Skating", Sandra Stevenson, 1984
256 "Kathy Casey," Terri Milner Tarquini, "The Professional Skater" magazine, November/December 2019
257 "Great, Big Wonderful Whirl", Jeannette Bruce, "Sports Illustrated" magazine, February 14, 1977
258 "Jr. Worlds", Howard Bass, "Skating" magazine, March 1978
259 "The BBC Book of Skating", Sandra Stevenson, 1984

triple Lutz in competition were Canada's Kay Thomson and France's Agnes Gosselin. Gosselin landed a triple Lutz in combination at the 1983 European Championships[260]; Thomson did two triple Lutzes at the 1983 Canadian Championships[261] and became the first Canadian woman to land the jump in international competition at that year's World Championships in Helsinki.[262]

Brian Boitano and Adam Rippon - two brilliant American skaters whose careers were separated by decades - both popularized unique variations to the Lutz jump. Brian Boitano's signature 'Tano was a Lutz with one arm outstretched overhead, while Adam Rippon's Rippon Lutz had both hands raised overhead.[263]

Though unsuccessful, the first skater to attempt a quad Lutz in competition was Evgeni Plushenko, at the 2001 Cup of Russia in St. Petersburg.[264] The first skater to

---
260 "1983 European Championships", Howard Bass, "Skating" magazine, April 1983
261 "Canadian Championships", Frank Nowosad, "Skating" magazine, April 1983
262 Video footage
263 Ibid
264 Ibid

successfully perform the quad Lutz in competition was America's Brandon Mroz. After landing the jump successfully at a domestic competition in Colorado Springs in 2011, Mroz repeated the feat at that year's NHK Trophy in Japan.[265]

The first skater to land a quad Lutz in an ISU Championship was Boyang Jin, at the 2016 Four Continents Championships.[266] The first woman to land a quad Lutz at an ISU Championship was Anna Shcherbakova, at the 2020 European Championships[267], though Alexandra Trusova was the first to do the jump in an international competition, in a Junior Grand Prix event in Armenia in the autumn of 2018.[268]

---

265 "ISU Figure Skating Media Guide 2022/2023", International Skating Union
266 "2016 Four Continents", Tatjana Flade, "International Figure Skating" magazine, February 24, 2016
267 "Alena Kostornaia wins European Figure Skating Championships in Russian '3A' clean sweep", Ken Browne, Olympics.com, January 26, 2020
268 "ISU Figure Skating Media Guide 2022/2023", International Skating Union

The Axel

The Axel is the most difficult of the edge jumps, taking off from the left forward outside edge and landing on the back outside edge of the right foot.

The jump was first presented in an international competition in January of 1882, the Internationale Pres-Figuren-Eislaufen von Amateurs competition[269] in Vienna, Austria, by Norwegian skater Axel Paulsen. Whereas most of the other competitors in the event presented complex special figures of their own design, Paulsen opted to focus his effort on a singular jump. Robert Büchter recounted that when Paulsen (a speed skater) did his jump for the first time, "He skated backwards, turned, then jumped from a V with 1 1/2 rotations about 1 meters and landed on the other foot in almost a deep squat, and rising from the squat, skated a large spiraling arc."[270] A review of the competition noted, "The

---

[269] "Special-Programm für das Internationale Presi-Figuren-Eislaufen von Amateurs", "Allgemeine Sport-Zeitung", June 30, 1881
[270] "Theorie und Praxis des Kunstlaufes am Eise", Gilbert Fuchs, 1926

public applauded furiously when Axel Paulsen at the end of a figure jumped backwards to a considerable distance and then finished with a pirouette which looked like something turned round by the whirlwind."[271]

Robert Büchter's description of Axel Paulsen's jump inspired German skater Gilbert Fuchs to develop his forward take-off 'Drehsprung', with an entrance from a crouched position. Fuchs was adamant that his jump had "nothing in common [with the Axel] but the 1 1/2 rotation", though by descriptions it was likely a different interpretation of the same jump. Irving Brokaw noted that Fuchs' variation was performed thusly: "Begin by some short steps on inside back in the form of a circle, holding the arms outstretched to prepare for a good balance; come next to a forward cross roll; the body must now begin to be well 'screwed' around to get the skater into position to properly alight. The skater now sinks well on the employed knee, while obtaining a purchase on the ice by digging well in on the forward and outside edge of the blade; then by a turn in the air for one-

---
[271] "Our Vienna Letter", "Sydney Morning Herald", January 26, 1882

and-a-half revolutions he alights gracefully on the outside edge of the other foot."[272] Fuchs explained, "The upper body and arm are shot up, the rotation takes place in the air, landing on the right back outside edge in a spiral. I've seen other runners lead in with threes to gain more momentum. The disadvantage of this... is that the rotation is often so strong that it cannot be parried after the jump and the arc turns into involuntary turns after the jump." He demonstrated his 'Drehsprung' for the first time in competition at the German and Austrian Championships in Darmstadt (1896) and in the special figures event at the World Championships in St. Petersburg in 1896.[273]

Canadian skater George Meagher soon developed his own variation of a forward take-off jump. He described his 'Meagher Jump' as "jumping from the outside forward on one foot, making a complete revolution in the air, and alighting forward on the same foot, finishing in this position."[274]

During the Edwardian era, Axel jumps were

---
[272] "The Art of Skating", Irving Brokaw, 1915
[273] "Theorie und Praxis des Kunstlaufes am Eise", Gilbert Fuchs, 1926
[274] "Guide to Artistic Skating", George Meagher, 1919

performed in competition by a handful of skaters, including Austria's Ernst Herz and Max Bohatsch.[275] Dorothy Greenhough Smith, the winner of the Swedish Challenge Cup in 1908 and 1911 and wife of the editor of the magazine that published Sir Arthur Conan Doyle's "Sherlock Holmes" stories[276], was the first woman to perform the jump in the Olympic Games in 1908.[277] Captain T.D. Richardson, who skated with Greenhough Smith at Prince's Skating Club in London, recalled that she "could jump it with complete nonchalance - complete with ankle length skirt, hat and very high skates indeed."[278] It should be noted that German accounts of this period differentiated between the Axel and 1 1/2 'Sprung Wendung' (jump turn), suggesting that Fuchs and Paulsen's jumps were still viewed as two separate ones.[279]

Several variations of the Axel and technique changes were pioneered in the first half of the twentieth century. The Böckl Jump, described

---

275 "Kunst des Eislaufs: praktische Winke", George Helfrich, 1922
276 "Death of Mr. Greenhough Smith", "The Western Daily Press and Bristol Mirror", January 15, 1935
277 "Skating: The Olympic Competitions", Geoffrey Hall-Say, "The Field", October 31, 1908
278 "Ice Skating", Captain T.D. Richardson, 1956
279 "Eissportbuch", Fritz Reuel, 1928

in 1919 by George Meagher[280] and popularized by World Champion Willy Böckl in the 1920s, took off from the right forward inside edge and landed on the right back outside edge.[281] Cecilia Colledge popularized an Inside Axel taking off from the left forward outside edge and landing on the left back inside.[282] One-foot Axels were being performed in the 1920s by Austrian skater Ernst Oppacher.[283] Gustave Lussi re-worked the technique of the Axel so that skaters 'checked' the landing and developed the delayed Axel[284] which he taught to Dorothy Hamill many years later.[285] Before this, many skaters would do three turns out of the jump.[286] In Austria and Germany in the late 1920s and early 1930s, an Axel variation called the Kadettensprung rose to prominence. It was described as a "leaping triple step of English origin", beginning on the left forward outside edge and ending on a

---

280 "Guide to Artistic Skating", George Meagher, 1919
281 "Jumps: Description and History", Hildegarde Balmain, Pierre Brunet and Carrie Reynolds, "Skating" magazine, December 1943
282 "Another Collection of Jumps", "Skating" magazine, January 1944
283 "Sports Illustrated Figure Skating: Championship Techniques", John 'Misha' Petkevich, 1989
284 "Biographical Sketch of Gustave Lussi", Cecily Morrow
285 Video footage
286 Ibid

right back outside. "The English origin" may well be traced to World Champion Megan Taylor's father Phil, who performed the jump in an exhibition at the Wiener Eislaufverein in Vienna in the spring of 1927.[287] The Kadettensprung was later demonstrated by Hilde Holovsky and Felix Kaspar[288] and included in the free skating program of Karl Schäfer.[289]

As late as the 1940s, it was believed that different Axel techniques constituted different jumps altogether. The Spot Axel, which was described as "mainly [being] used in theatrical performances" was seen as a "practically stationary" jump entered from a left backward inside edge, whereas the Flying or English Axel was a "low and fast" jump where the skater "travels over the ice quite a distance before landing."[290]

Felix Kaspar and Freddie Tomlins were famous for the height they achieved on their

---

287 "Eissport", "Linzer Tages-Post", March 6, 1927
288 "Schaulaufpremiere auf dem Heumarkt", "Der Montag", December 14, 1931
289 "Karl Schäfer in Linz", "Alpenländische Morgen Zeitung", January 15, 1934
290 "Jumps: Description and History", Hildegarde Balmain, Pierre Brunet and Carrie Reynolds, "Skating" magazine, December 1943

jumps. ISU Historian Benjamin T. Wright recalled, "The Skating Club of Boston invited Tomlins to come to our carnival in 1939, just before the War. He was an extraordinary jumper, and we measured. He did a double Salchow that was twenty-five feet long. He was a short guy and his feet were above the boards. Coincidentally, the year before, Felix Kaspar came and he was a little guy too. He was the kind of guy that'd get up in the air and do a flying Axel thirty feet long and four feet high! With that skill [and different skates], it was obvious they could have done quads."[291]

Two of the first people to demonstrate the Axel on rollers were actually accomplished figure skaters. In 1940, Skippy Baxter gave an exhibition where did a double Salchow and ten Axels in a row. At the previous year's U.S. Roller Skating Championships, the senior skaters were only doing Salchows, loops and flips. Hedy Stenuf also performed the Axel and double jumps on both ice and rollers during this period.[292]

Doing a succession of Axel's in a row was a

---

291 Interview with Benjamin T. Wright, March 12, 2017
292 "History of Roller Skating", James Turner, 1975

popular feature in the free skating performances of many top skaters during this period, perhaps most famously those given by Olympian and actress Belita Jepson-Turner.[293]

Experimentation with the double Axel began before World War II. Czechoslovakian skater Otto Gold attempted a double Axel at the second European Championships of the 1929/1930 season, but performed the jump using the technique of the time, landing in a deep pirouette.[294] The first skater to execute the double Axel using the modern technique in an international competition was Dick Button, at the 1948 Winter Olympic Games, in St. Moritz, Switzerland.[295] Just over a month later, his young American teammate Johnny Lettengarver landed the jump in an exhibition in Bournemouth, England.[296] Hungary's Ede Király was working on the double Axel around the same time, landing one in an exhibition he gave at the British Championships at Wembley in December of

---

293 Interview with Bob Turk, March 17, 2016
294 "Die Genese des Eiskunstlaufens als Prozess der Versportung und struktureller Veränderungen im Wettkampfsystem sowie der Leistungsentwicklung", Dr. Matthias Hampe, Humanwissenschaftlichen Fakultät der Universität Potsdam, 2010
295 "Dick Button on Skates", Dick Button, 1956
296 "News from the Rinks", "Skating World" magazine, April 1948

1948.[297] Not to be outdone, Ron Ludington became the first man to land the double Axel/double loop combination on rollers.[298] By 1952, when Button won his second Olympic gold medal and landed the first triple loop in competition, a handful of men were attempting double Axels. Button did four - one at the start of his program and three in a row near the end.[299]

It was also in the early 1950s that women started attempting double Axels in competition. Tenley Albright was the first to attempt it.[300] She stood up on the jump at the 1951 World Championships[301] and 1954 U.S. Championships[302] but sometimes cheated the landing of the jump.[303] It was Albright's teammate Carol Heiss who set the gold

---

297 "British Amateur Figure Skating Championships", Dennis L. Bird (writing under the pseudonym John Noel), "Skating World" magazine, January 1949
298 "History of Roller Skating", James Turner, 1975
299 "Olympic Diary", Dennis L. Bird (writing under the pseudonym John Noel), "Skating World" magazine, March 1952
300 "Die Genese des Eiskunstlaufens als Prozess der Versportung und struktureller Veränderungen im Wettkampfsystem sowie der Leistungsentwicklung", Dr. Matthias Hampe, Humanwissenschaftlichen Fakultät der Universität Potsdam, 2010
301 "Comments on the World Championships", "Skating" magazine, May 1951
302 ""United States Championships", Sevy Von Sonn, "Skating" magazine, March 1954
303 Video footage

standard for the double Axel in the 1950s, landing it cleanly for the first of many times in international competition at the 1955 World Championships in Vienna.[304] Heiss' mastery of the double Axel and repertoire of double jumps played a key part in her dominance of the sport in the years leading up to her Olympic gold medal win in 1960.

British Movietone footage released in September of 1957 showcased David Jenkins performing a beautiful triple Axel on the famous outdoor rink in Sun Valley, Idaho.[305] He stopped working on the jump that winter, not long after landing it in Sun Valley.[306] Like Donald Jackson, who performed the first triple Lutz in competition five years later, Jenkins' accomplishment was light years ahead of its time. In an interview with Allison Manley for The Manleywoman SkateCast in 2011, Jenkins recalled, "Until the time I went to medical school, I'd pretty much accomplished the triple flip, and was working on the triple Axel to the point where I could

---

304 "The Championships of the World", "Skating" magazine, April 1955
305 Video footage
306 "Spotlighting the World Champions: 1957 Triple Titleholder's", Edith E. Ray and Freda Alexander, "Skating" magazine, June 1957

land it about fifty percent of the time on a good day. That wasn't the sort of statistic that would lead me to put it in a program yet, but when I went to medical school I really did not have the time to train on those sorts of advances... I was the only person really doing triples at the time, and there was no advantage to me trying to do the triple Axel in competition because no one else was doing triples... I spent a lot of time on all the triples before I could master them, and I approached the triple Axel the same way because there wasn't anyone who could coach me. Edi [Scholdan] was no help with that. It was just a frontier. He was a very good school figures coach and very good at tearing things apart, but not so good about putting them together and learning from that, so I pretty much relied on myself. We didn't have film or video or things you could watch in those days, so you couldn't really learn from seeing yourself. For me, it was just repetition until the timing became a part of you. It was just trial and error."[307]

Gordon McKellen Jr. was the first skater to

---

[307] Interview with David Jenkins, Allison Manley, The Manleywoman SkateCast, April 7, 2011

attempt the triple Axel in international competition at the 1974 World Championships in Munich. He landed half a dozen in practice sessions and warm-ups, but fell on his attempt in the free skate.[308] He accomplished it during the exhibitions of that event[309], as well as the exhibitions at the 1975 U.S. Championships.[310]

Robin Cousins showed up at the National Skating Association's Skater's Ball in 1977 with a sprained wrist. He admitted he had done it while working on a triple Axel.[311] Cousins landed the jump in practice – Carlo Fassi even caught one on videotape[312] – but he never attempted it in competition.

Japan's Mitsuru Matsumura reportedly landed the triple Axel in a regional event in Japan in the autumn of 1977[313] but took a fall on the

---

308 "Worlds '74", Howard Bass, "Skating" magazine, May 1974
309 Interview with Frazer Ormondroyd, January 4, 2023; Video footage
310 "Nationals '75: ... And That's the Way It Was", Sue Schauppner, "Skating" magazine, April 1975
311 "Robin Cousins: Skating For Gold", Robin Cousins and Howard Bass, 1980
312 "Robin Cousins: The Authorized Biography", Martha Lowder Kimball, 1998
313 "Japanese National Championships", Junko Hiramatsu, "Skating" magazine, February 1978

jump at the 1978 World Championships in Ottawa.[314] West Germany's Rudi Cerne was also unsuccessful in his attempt.[315] Canada's Vern Taylor was recognized at those Championships as the first skater to accomplish a triple Axel in an ISU Championship. ISU President Jacques Favart reviewed videotape of Taylor's historic jump in slow motion to verify that the jump was rotated and landed on the correct edge.[316] Favart remarked, "Of course, he over-rotated a little on the landing and it was not perfect but it was a triple Axel, there's no doubt about that."[317] Dick Button, commentating for American television coverage of the 1981 World Championships in Hartford, acknowledged Taylor's jump in 1978, but praised Brian Orser's clean triple Axel, stating, "A triple Axel was done once before in a World Championships... but never has one been done as well as this."[318]

---

314 Interview with Frazer Ormondroyd, January 4, 2023; Video footage
315 "Charles Tickner wins men's skating title", Nora McCabe, "The Globe and Mail", March 10, 1978
316 "First triple Axel ever", "The Albertan", March 10, 1978
317 "Toronto's Vern Taylor makes skating history", "The Sault Star", March 10, 1978
318 Video footage

In the late 1970s, Switzerland's Denise Biellmann and Yugoslavia's Sanda Dubravčić made history as the first women to land the double Axel/half-loop/triple Salchow and double Axel/triple toe-loop combinations in international competition.[319]

America's Tiffany Chin is believed to be the first woman to conquer the triple Axel[320], but she never attempted the jump in competition. Japan's Midori Ito began working on triple Axels in practice in 1985, but gave up on practicing the jump for a time after breaking her leg.[321] She attempted the jump for the first time in international competition in the autumn of 1988 at Skate America in Portland, Maine, stepping out of the landing.[322] She made history at that season's NHK Trophy[323], Japanese Championships[324] and World Championships[325], landing the jump for the first time in national, international and World

---

319 "Die Genese des Eiskunstlaufens als Prozess der Versportung und struktureller Veränderungen im Wettkampfsystem sowie der Leistungsentwicklung", Dr. Matthias Hampe, Humanwissenschaftlichen Fakultät der Universität Potsdam, 2010
320 Video footage
321 "Midori Ito", Deb Vestal, "Skating" magazine, October 1988
322 Video footage
323 Ibid
324 "News Briefs", "Skating" magazine, December 1988
325 Video footage

competition. In 1991 at Skate America, Tonya Harding made history as the first woman to land two triple Axels in one combination, as well as the first triple Axel in the short program in combination.[326] The first Canadian woman to attempt the jump in competition was Lisa Sargeant, at Skate Electric in England in the autumn of 1990.[327] She landed the jump in practice but not consistently, yet continued to attempt it in competition for several years.[328]

In 2018, Artur Dmitriev Jr. - the Russian-born son of Olympic Gold Medallist pairs skater Artur Dmitriev - made history by attempting the quad Axel for the first time at the Rostelecom Cup in Moscow. Four years later, two-time Olympic Gold Medallist Yuzuru Hanyu made a risky attempt at the jump at the Winter Olympic Games in Beijing.[329] The honour of being the first skater to land a quad Axel in competition in 2022 went to Ilia Malinin, the American-born son of Uzbek Olympians Tatiana Malinina and Roman

---
326 Ibid
327 "Sargeant masters triple in practice", Marty Knack, "Edmonton Journal", September 1990
328 "Learning To Relax: Sargeant-Driscoll more positive", Lori Ewing, "Calgary Herald", January 16, 1993
329 Video footage

Skorniakov.[330] For decades, many believed the jump was impossible and for many skaters, it likely is... underscoring the courage, conviction and talent of the few skaters who have even dared to attempt it.

> ### AXEL-ORATE YOUR KNOWLEDGE
>
> Robin Cousins set a Guinness World Record in 1983 for the longest Axel on skates, reaching 5.81 meters.
>
> Long-time skating fans will remember Jozef Sabovčík's delayed Tuck Axel as one of most exciting elements performed in professional skating competitions of the 1990s.

---

[330] "American Ilia Malinin, 17, lands 1st-ever quad axel in competition", Dave Skretta, CBC News, September 15, 2022

The Walley

The Walley is a full rotation 'reverse' jump where the skater jumps from a back inside edge, makes a full rotation and lands on the back outside edge of the same foot. Like the toeless or 'Diesel' Lutz, the skater rotates against the edge. An underappreciated jump in recent years, the Walley was once a staple in free skating programs. It has fallen by the wayside since the introduction of the IJS because it doesn't receive any points as a jump element. Instead, it is considered a transitional movement.[331]

For many years, there has been some confusion surrounding who created the Walley jump. In fact, about half a dozen names pop up when you take a deep dive into the history of the Walley.

The obvious, of course, would be the namesake of the jump. Minnesota-born Nathan 'Nate' Walley. Walley worked as a

---

331 "Judging System Technical Panel Handbook: Single Skating, 2022/2023", International Skating Union

jobber in a machinist shop in Minneapolis[332] before becoming one of the first professional instructors in California.[333] Nate moved to England in 1934, where he won the British Open Professional title twice consecutively, defeating the likes of Howard Nicholson, Jacques Gerschwiler and Edi Scholdan. Back in those days, the competition consisted of both school figures and free skating - not something we think of today when it comes to professional events.[334] It was his spectacular free skating that helped him prevail on both occasions. While in England, he taught at Streatham Ice Rink for a time, passed the National Skating Association's Gold test and appeared in the ice revue "A Night in Cafe Montmartre"[335] with Phil Taylor and a young Freddie Tomlins, who was his pupil for a short period.[336] He later coached in Australia[337], Canada[338] and the United States[339].

---

332 United States Census, 1930
333 "Rockers and Counters", "Skating" magazine, May 1934
334 "The Almanac of Professional Figure Skating Competitions", Ryan Stevens, May 18, 2021
335 "Attractions at Streatham: London Championship Game and 'Cafe Montmartre'", "Croydon Times", March 31, 1934
336 "A Trans-Atlantic View of Recent European Activities", Maribel Yerxa Vinson, "Skating" magazine, March 1935
337 "Glaciarium: Spectacular Revue", "The Age" (Melbourne, Victoria), August 23, 1937
338 "Sister Act", "Maclean's" magazine, December 15, 1943
339 "Lake Placid Summer Skating", Polly Blodgett, "Skating" magazine,

Walley also made another very important contribution to figure skating during his lifetime. He collaborated with the USFSA on a comprehensive table of jumps and spins, categorizing everything from the well-known Axel and Salchow to the often underappreciated toeless Lutz and one-and-a-half flip. This table, adapted and republished around the world in dozens of languages, helped expand the possibilities of free skating for countless skaters and coaches.[340]

In 1934, Scottish skater T. Patrick C. 'Pat' Low won a senior men's event held in conjunction with the European Championships in Seefeld, Austria[341] during a raging blizzard.[342] Walley and Low were both training in England that year. Low was working on a full-rotation toeless jump from the right backward inside edge to the left backward inside edge.[343] His jump was of course different to the Walley, as the landing was on an inside edge. It is unknown whether Nate Walley consciously

---

November 1935
340 "Proper Credit", Theresa Weld Blanchard, "Skating" magazine, June 1958
341 "Karl Schäfer wieder Europameister", "Wiener Sporttagblatt", January 22, 1934
342 "London Asides", Pamela Murray, "The Sketch", May 2, 1934
343 "Krasobruslení", Vladimir Koudelka, 1936

decided to start doing the jump with an outside edge landing or if it just evolved naturally that way, but he was responsible for popularizing the jump in North America[344] and by the early forties, it had already started popping up in the free skating programs of American skaters.[345]

Two of Nate Walley's coaching colleagues, Maribel Vinson Owen and Robert S. Ogilvie, had similar takes on how the Walley came to be. Vinson Owen mused, "The so-called 'Walley' jump, which was in fact originated by an English India-rubber-man named Pat Low, a most amazing fellow who could jump from any edge in any direction and land on his feet like a cat. Nathan Walley, however, introduced it to this country, and so Americans and Canadians have quite naturally given it his name."[346] Ogilvie remarked, "During a quiet public session... Nate Walley and Pat Low were skating on the same ice. With all due respect to Mr. Walley, I cannot help feeling he might have been influenced by watching Mr. Low doing his

---

344 "Turner's Turn", Eugene Turner, "Skating" magazine, April 1984
345 "Meet the Champions", "Skating" magazine, March 1941
346 "Maribel Y. Vinson's Advanced Figure Skating", Maribel Vinson Owen, 1940

specialties, one of which bore a marked resemblance to the Walley. But then, my English background may have made me a little biased."[347]

The jump's origins may also be traced to Austria. NSA Historian Dennis L. Bird recalled that on the Continent the Walley was known "as the 'Distler' - presumably after the Austrian skater Dr. Hugo Distler, runner-up in the 1927 European [Championships]. Which of them really originated it I don't know."[348] Austrian-born coach Walter Arian asserted that Olympic Gold Medallist Karl Schäfer was working on a similar jump around the same time.[349]

Part of the confusion surrounding the Walley and Pat Low jumps was perpetuated by the fact that figure skating rulebooks listed the two jumps as the same for decades.[350] Interestingly, roller skating manuals have

---

347 "The Walley", Robert S. Ogilvie, "The Professional Skater" magazine, September/October 2013
348 "The Art of Jumping: A Spectator's Guide – II: Jumps from a Backward Edge", Dennis L. Bird (writing under pseudonym John Noel), "Skating World" magazine, February 1961
349 "Jumps: Description and History," "Skating" magazine, December 1943
350 Canadian Figure Skating Association Rulebook, 1984

consistently differentiated between the two jumps.[351]

The Walley and Pat Low jumps were seen as something of a novelty. In 1936, Czechoslovakian skater Vladimir Koudelka remarked, "They are rarely carried out. I've seen them laugh at Patrick Low. [They say the jump] doesn't look aesthetic and they're just a kind of curiosity in jumps."[352]

In the 1950s, Hungarian Champion György Czakó was credited with developing a variation on the Walley jump. In a 2016 interview, he explained, "We were out in [the] Soviet Union to 'change experience' at the time when the Soviet figure skating was in [its] infancy. When we were out there the second time, I noticed that the eighty-second jump in a register of a Russian coach is the Czakó jump. Then at the Olympic Games, it turned out that this jump was invented in the West as well and was called Robertson, somewhere else Walley." The difference between the Czakó jump and the Robertson jump, as Czakó explained, is in the take-off:

---

351 "Roller Free Skating: Singles and Pairs", United States Amateur Confederation of Roller Skating, 1980
352 "Krasobruslení", Vladimir Koudelka, 1936

the Czakó from a crossover, the Robertson from a serpentine.[353]

Over the years, double Walley's have been performed both on roller and ice skates, but they have been few and far between. Without the toe assist, the rotation against the edge on this jump makes multiple rotations of this jump extremely challenging. Atoy Wilson, Gary Beacom, Robert Wagenhoffer, Jozef Sabovčík and Brendan Kerry are among the few to master the rare jump.[354] One of the first skaters documented to have done a double Pat Low jump was Jimmy Grogan in 1947.[355] Robert S. Ogilvie noted, "A handful of skaters have achieved it but largely from their academic interest in the jump. I have, however, seen the double performed very creditably by Mr. Colin Van der Veen during his free skating program at the 1993 U.S. Nationals. Fortunately, I was taping the event at the time so have been able to refer back to it for confirmation. I think it took everyone by surprise and the commentators received it in a rare moment of absolute silence, in fact,

---
353 Interview with György Czakó, February 24, 2016
354 Video footage
355 "U.S. Championships Go West", Mary L. Paige, "Skating" magazine, April 1947

they never referred to it either at the time or since. To the best of my knowledge, this was the first time the double had been performed in a national or international competition."[356]

Unfortunately, as long as the IJS continues to exclude the Walley and Pat Low jumps from the list of scoring jump elements, they face the same fate as the Dodo bird.

---

356 "The Walley", Robert S. Ogilvie, "The Professional Skater" magazine, September/October 2013

Side-by-Side Jumps

In the "early days", pairs programs consisted solely of dance steps, field figures and spins. Two of the first duos noted to have included small jumps in their programs before The Great War were Grete Bartel and Alois Wilschek of Troppau and Hedwig and Dr. Hugo Winzer of Dresden. These were small hops included in combined figures.[357]

1908 Olympic Gold Medallists Anna Hübler and Heinrich Burger also pushed boundaries during the Edwardian era, with a small assisted three jump in their program. However, Burger cautioned, "Due consideration should be given [to] the fact that pirouettes and jumps impair the rhythm. Whoever can succeed in skating this kind of figure to the music, however, may rightly claim that his pair-skating should score high, on the difficulty of it."[358]
Side-by-side jumping was first really

---
357 "Kunstfertigkeit im Eislaufen", Robert Holletschek, 1925
358 "Pair-Skating", Heinrich Burger, in "The Art of Skating", Irving Brokaw, 1915

popularized during the era of the Charleston, when attitudes about the validity of shadow skating[359] began to change. Footage exists of Americans Beatrix Loughran and Sherwin Badger performing side-by-side single jumps at the 1928 Winter Olympic Games in St. Moritz.[360]

During the 1920s and 1930s, side-by-side Axels were far from common, but they weren't non-existent. Since Gustave Lussi had taught both Constance and Montgomery Wilson the Axel[361], the possibility exists that the Canadian siblings may have been the first or one of the first pairs to perform side-by-side Axels. The 1936 Olympic Gold Medallists Maxi Herber and Ernst Baier usually 'only' attempted solo flips, loops and waltz jumps, but they did include Axels in their program more than once[362]. Their performance of the jump at the 1934 World Championships is believed to be a first at an ISU Championship.[363] A similar pair from

---

359 "Ice-Skating: A History", Nigel Brown, 1959
360 Video footage
361 "Biographical Sketch of Gustave Lussi", Cecily Morrow
362 "Drei klare Siege in den Kunstlauf-Europameisterschaften", "Wiener Sporttagblatt", January 27, 1936
363 "Die Genese des Eiskunstlaufens als Prozess der Versportung und struktureller Veränderungen im Wettkampfsystem sowie der

Canada, Dorothy and Hazel Caley, also mastered the one-and-a-half revolution jump.[364] Maribel Vinson and George 'Geddy' Hill 'only' went for side-by-side Lutzes in their program at the 1936 Olympics.[365]

Maribel Vinson Owen stressed the importance of side-by-side jumps being performed as close together as possible, but advised, "When Guy [Owen] and I were making the Grantland Rice technique film 'Good Skates', we did a side-by-side flip jump so close that we crashed in mid-air - and that I do not advocate! However, anything less than a crash is all to the good, and if you and your partner can't pull your jumps off without a wide space between you, you had better leave them out until you acquire the knack - or the courage."[366]

Before and during World War II, side-by-side jumps were often featured in combination

---

Leistungsentwicklung", Dr. Matthias Hampe, Humanwissenschaftlichen Fakultät der Universität Potsdam, 2010

364 "Maribel Y. Vinson's Advanced Figure Skating", Maribel Vinson Owen, 1940
365 "The Fourth Olympic Winter Games", Theresa Weld Blanchard, "Skating" magazine, April 1936
366 "Maribel Y. Vinson's Advanced Figure Skating", Maribel Vinson Owen, 1940

with dance steps and not as 'standalone' feature elements. U.S. Champions Doris Schubach and Walter Noffke cautioned pairs against "many single or separate jumps"[367] in a program, as they were not demonstrative of quality pairs skating. Schubach remarked, "If the two skaters find that they jump from the same foot and that their styles are similar, then they should include a few in their program. Do not forget, however, that you are not exhibiting your ability as single skaters, but rather as two people skating as one. Do not let your program appear as if it could just as easily be skated by one person as by two."[368] Canadians Sheila and Ross Smith took an opposite approach during Wartime, peppering their program with solo loop, Lutz and Axel jumps.[369]

During the first half of the twentieth century, it wasn't uncommon for pairs to execute waltz jumps hand-in-hand to gain speed at corners[370] or perform 'passing' jumps in

---

[367] "Pair Skating As We See It", Doris Schubach and Walter Noffke, "Skating" magazine, March 1943
[368] "In The Editor's Mail", "Skating" magazine, October 1943
[369] "Meet the Canadian Champions", Mavis Berry Daane, Naomi Slater, "Skating" magazine, March 1944
[370] "Pair Skating and Dancing on Ice", Rosemarie Stewart and Robert S. Dench, 1943

unison which weren't side-by-side. Maribel Vinson Owen recalled, "Norah McCarthy and Ralph McCreath jumped in a small separating figure and held their landing into a controlled meeting... Joan Tozzer and Bernard Fox did Salchow jumps past each other, a particularly rhythmic move, as the sway of their bodies as they approached on the rather long preparation was interesting and the dip for the jump was timed so that they passed each other actually in the air."[371] A novel idea proposed by Stewart and Dench was the inclusion of side-by-side jumps of a different type. They remarked, "It is not necessary that you both do the same jumps at the same time. If you find that each of you do a certain jump better than the other, then by all means combine the two different jumps. For example, the lady may do a split while the man does a Lutz, and the combination is a very effective one."[372]

There has long been a debate as to which pairs team was the first to perform side-by-side double jumps. Canadians have long

---

[371] "Maribel Y. Vinson's Advanced Figure Skating", Maribel Vinson Owen, 1940
[372] "Pair Skating and Dancing on Ice", Rosemarie Stewart and Robert S. Dench, 1943

asserted that Suzanne Morrow and Wallace Distelmeyer performed double jumps at the 1948 Winter Olympic Games and World Championships, while Germans have claimed that the first side-by-side double jumps were performed by 1952 Olympic Gold Medallists Ria (Baran) and Paul Falk.[373] Video footage of Baran and Falk's performances that exist in Das Bundesarchiv only show them performing side-by-side waltz jumps and Salchows,[374] while the Morrow-Francis and Distelmeyer claim was backed up by Canadian coach Sheldon Galbraith, who was of course in Switzerland in 1948 as Barbara Ann Scott's coach[375] and the research of German skating historian Dr. Matthias Hampe.[376] Morrow and Distelmeyer's successors, Marlene Smith and Donald Gilchrist performed solo double toe-loops and Salchows.[377] Footage exists of Americans Carole Ormaca and Robin Greiner

---

373 "Paarlauf-Olympiasieger Paul Falk wird 90", "DerWesten", December 19, 2011
374 Video footage
375 "Figure Skating: A Celebration", Beverley Smith, 1994
376 "Die Genese des Eiskunstlaufens als Prozess der Versportung und struktureller Veränderungen im Wettkampfsystem sowie der Leistungsentwicklung", Dr. Matthias Hampe, Humanwissenschaftlichen Fakultät der Universität Potsdam, 2010
377 "Times have really changed: The national figure skating championships are the Big Daddy of Canadian amateur sports gatherings, not anything like it was at the old Minto Skating Club in 1949", Martin Cleary, "The Ottawa Citizen", January 21, 1999

performing side-by-side double Salchows at the 1956 Winter Olympics in Cortina d'Ampezzo and Canadians Barbara Wagner and Bob Paul performing side-by-side double toe-loops at the 1960 Winter Olympics in Squaw Valley.[378]

Though side-by-side jumps had been included in pairs programs for decades by the early sixties, they were still considered a novelty - not a standard or 'expected' element. Debbi Wilkes recalled, "Back in those days side-by-side jumps were not key elements in a pair program. I think the most we ever did was maybe a double Salchow. What we did were all the technical pair elements."[379]

That said, there were certainly a handful of teams that pushed the envelope in this area. The Jelineks faltered on their attempt at solo double Axels at the 1962 World Championships[380] but landed a wide range of other double jumps, including the Lutz.[381] The

---
378 Video footage
379 Interview with Debbi Wilkes, June 2019
380 Video footage
381 "Die Genese des Eiskunstlaufens als Prozess der Versportung und struktureller Veränderungen im Wettkampfsystem sowie der Leistungsentwicklung", Dr. Matthias Hampe, Humanwissenschaftlichen Fakultät der Universität Potsdam, 2010

same year, Dorothyann Nelson and Pieter Kollen and Milada Kubíková and Jaroslav Votruba both successfully performed double flips.[382] Nelson and Kollen's double flips were side-by-side but were very intentionally not in unison[383], whereas the Jelineks attempted the double Axel in unison, but not side-by-side.[384] Russian[385] and American[386] sources have both claimed Nina and Stanislav Zhuk attempted solo double Axels. A report in "Skating magazine" noted that The Zhuks were unsuccessful in their attempt at the 1960 Olympics[387].

By the late 1960s, the standard among the top pairs teams in the world was to include more than one side-by-side double jump in a free skating program. These were still usually Salchows, toe-loops or loops. After all, when the compulsory short program was

---

382 "The Worlds Day by Day", Jane Vaughn Sullivan, "Skating" magazine, May 1962
383 "The United States Championships", Evelyn L. Carroll, Dr. Robert Claflin and Dorothy H. Albert, "Skating" magazine, April 1962
384 Video footage
385 "Принес 138 медалей СССР, его обвиняли в аморальном поведении и писали доносы в ЦК. История тренера Станислава Жука", Elizabeta Glinkina, "Sport24", January 4, 2021
386 "The Big Red Machine: The Rise and Fall of Soviet Olympic Champions", Yuri Brokhin, 1978
387 "The Olympics: 1960", Edith E. Ray, "Skating" magazine, April 1960

introduced for pairs in 1964, the only required side-by-side jumps were the Axel and double Salchow.[388] Soviets Tamara Moskvina and Alexei Mishin[389], Americans Barbara Brown and Douglas Berndt and East Germans Manuela Groß and Uwe Kagelmann[390] pushed the limit with side-by-side double Lutzes.

Russian sources have claimed Irina Rodnina and Alexei Ulanov were the first team to successfully land side-by-side double Axels, at the 1969 European Championships in Garmisch-Partenkirchen.[391] Video footage reveals that Rodnina and Ulanov did not attempt double Axels at that event or either the 1970 European or World Championships. At the 1971 European Championships, Rodnina cheated the landing and Ulanov fell. At the 1971 World Championships, they stood up on the landings but commentator Eva Pawlik was quick to point out that the jumps were not clean. This was again the case

---

388 "Pair Skating: New Compulsory Program", International Skating Union Communication No. 350, 1964
389 Video footage
390 "Europeans", Nigel Brown and Sandra Stevenson, "Skating" magazine, April 1971
391 "Триумфальные победы Ирины Родниной", Peoples.ru - Journal 'Lyudi', May 23, 2016

when they attempted the jump at the 1972 European Championships and World Championships. They opted not to include the double Axels at the 1972 Winter Olympic Games. Rodnina achieved the side-by-side double Axel for the first time in an ISU Championship at the 1973 European Championships with her second partner, Aleksandr Zaitsev.[392]

Six-time Polish Champions Janina Poremska and Piotr Sczypa were unsuccessful in their attempt at solo double Axels at the 1970 European Championships in Leningrad.[393] A report from the 1972 Olympic Games noted that the only pair to land side-by-side double Axels were Americans Melissa and Mark Militano.[394] If this is correct, this would mean the first pair to land side-by-side double Axels in a major international competition may have been the Militano's.

By 1977, the side-by-side jumps in Irina Rodnina and Alexander Zaitsev's program

---

392 Interview with Frazer Ormondroyd, January 6, 2023; Video footage
393 Ibid
394 "XI Olympic Winter Games", Kikuko Minami, "Skating" magazine, April 1972

were the double Axel, half loop/loop/double toe-loop combination, double flip, Axel and double Salchow series.[395] Tai Babilonia and Randy Gardner performed side-by-side double Axels, double loops and a split/two half loop/double Salchow series in 1979.[396]

Side-by-side triple jumps slowly started making their way into the pairs skating vocabulary in the 1970s. Americans Melissa and Mark Militano were unsuccessful in their attempt to be the first pair to perform side-by-side triple toe-loops at the 1975 World Championships in Colorado Springs.[397] Tracy and Scott Prussack landed side-by-side triple Salchows at the 1977 U.S. Championships in Hartford, Connecticut.[398]

Stanislav Zhuk's students Marina Cherkasova and Sergei Shakrai made history as the first pair to land side-by-side triple jumps in an ISU Championships when they landed triple

---

[395] "Pair Skating as Sport and Art", Tamara Moskvina and Igor Moskvin, International Skating Union, 1987
[396] Video footage
[397] "Die Genese des Eiskunstlaufens als Prozess der Versportung und struktureller Veränderungen im Wettkampfsystem sowie der Leistungsentwicklung", Dr. Matthias Hampe, Humanwissenschaftlichen Fakultät der Universität Potsdam, 2010
[398] "Nationals", Mary-Lucille Ager, "Skating" magazine, April 1977

toe-loops at the 1978 European Championships in Strasbourg. They fell short in their attempts at landing the groundbreaking element at both the 1978 and 1979 World Championships, then abandoned the element entirely.[399] Soviet teammates Irina Vorobieva and Igor Lisovsky landed side-by-side triple Salchows at the 1979 World Championships in Vienna.[400]

By 1980, the CFSA's Gold Pair Test required four different side-by-side jumps: either a double Axel or double Lutz, double flip, double loop and double Salchow.[401] However, the short program required element groups only prescribed a double Salchow, double toe-loop, double flip or double loop. By 1984, pairs were required to attempt two side-by-side jumps in their free skating programs.[402] Elena Valova and Oleg Vasiliev's winning free skate at the 1983 World Championships featured clean side-by-side triple toe-loops. By 1985, young Russian pairs like Ekaterina Gordeeva and Sergei Grinkov and Elena

---

399 Video footage
400 Interview with Frazer Ormondroyd, January 4, 2023; Video footage
401 Canadian Figure Skating Association Rulebook, 1980
402 Canadian Figure Skating Association Rulebook, 1984

Leonova and Gennadi Krasnitski also had side-by-side triple jumps in their repertoire. Canadians Cynthia Coull and Mark Rowsom dabbled with both side-by-side triple toe-loops and Salchows early in their career.[403]

Though other teams sporadically attempted high-risk side-by-side jumps in the early 1980s, it was really the Soviet powerhouse pairs - Valova and Vasiliev, Gordeeva and Grinkov and their teammates Larisa Selezneva and Oleg Makarov - who consistently upped the ante for difficulty during that era, setting the standard of needing at least a side-by-side double Axel to be competitive. Giving a sense of the technical evolution of side-by-side jumps during this period, Tamara Moskvina and Igor Moskvin noted, "In 1972 no program had a double Axel jump or a triple jump. In 1987 every [free] program had either a double Axel jump or a triple jump."[404]

Not long after the ISU passed a rule change in June 1994 that allowed pairs to attempt a triple jump in the short program[405], the side-

---
403 Video footage
404 "Pair Skating as Sport and Art", Tamara Moskvina and Igor Moskvin, International Skating Union, 1987
405 "Official Update: Elections, Eligibility top ISU Congress Agenda",

by-side triple toe-loop firmly replaced the double Axel as the benchmark. By this point, American pairs had been the ones leading the way in the side-by-side jump department. Kristi Yamaguchi and Rudy Galindo did side-by-side triple flips in opposite directions and Shelby Lyons and Brian Wells pushed the envelope by attempting side-by-side triple loops.[406]

Canada's Meagan Duhamel made history at the 2005 Canadian Championships in London, Ontario, performing the first side-by-side triple Lutz in competition with her partner Ryan Arnold. Duhamel remarked, "We didn't think it was going to end up being such a big deal. We knew the World Champions and the American Champions had been trying it for years. Ryan and I never looked at it as 'we're going to be the first ones'. We just both knew we were able to do it in singles, so we thought, 'Why not use it?' It has become a great advantage for us."[407] Side-by-side triple Lutzes became the trademark of Meagan Duhamel and Eric

---

John F. LeFevre, "Skating" magazine, August 1994
406 Video footage
407 'Duhamel makes triumphant return to home club', Jason Pirie, "Sudbury Star", March 28, 2005

Radford, whose mastery of the jumps set them far apart from the pack and helped them win Olympic medals and World titles.[408]

---

408 Video footage

Twist Lifts

A twist lift starts from a backward approach, with the woman picking her toe between the man's feet and the man lifting her to the full extension of his arms and making a half turn. The woman rotates and begins her 'free fall' until the man catches her around the waist and sets her on the ice[409] on a backward outside edge on one foot.[410] A common variation of the twist lift is the addition of a split on the first half turn.

The genesis of the twist lift can be traced back to before World War II. 1936 Olympic Gold Medallists Maxi Herber and Ernst Baier of Germany developed their Baier Lift[411] in the 1930s, a move reminiscent of a modern twist lift without a release.[412] Rosemarie Stewart and Bob Dench described two split lifts in their 1943 book "Pair Skating and

---

409 "What's New in Free Skating", Ron Ludington, "Skating" magazine, March 1969
410 "International Skating Union: Special Regulations & Technical Rules, Single & Pair Skating and Ice Dance 2022", International Skating Union
411 "What's New in Free Skating", Ron Ludington, "Skating" magazine, March 1969
412 Video footage

Dancing on Ice": the Half-Turn Split Lift and the Stewart Split Lift. The Half-Turn Split Lift was an assisted split jump, with both skaters skating face to face, the woman picking the toe of her free leg into the ice behind and jumping up into an assisted split position as the man lifted her. The Stewart Split Lift was described thusly: "The full-turn split lift was originated by Miss Stewart before the last Olympic Games when she was skating with Mr. Ernest Yates of England. It starts like the split lift, just described, but then both skaters make a complete revolution instead of a half-turn. The lady finishes on her backward-inside edge; the man on his forward inside. Both then take up a horizontal spiral position... The lady must prepare for her jump exactly as she would for a solo split jump. As she jumps, the man makes the lift and at the same time starts the turn."[413] Canadians Frances Dafoe and Norris Bowden worked with coach Sheldon Galbraith to develop the loop twist lift in the early 1950s.[414]

---

[413] "Pair Skating and Dancing on Ice", Rosemarie Stewart and Robert S. Dench, 1943
[414] "Reflections", Frances Dafoe, "Skating Through Time", February 1998

Until the early 1960s, the 'twist lift' and 'jump twist lift' were considered two separate elements. British Pathé newsreel footage shows Soviet pair Nina and Stanislav Zhuk performing a jump twist lift in Moscow in 1960.[415] A review of the 1961 North American Championships in Philadelphia noted that two pairs performed twist lifts, while winners Maria and Otto Jelinek performed a jump twist lift.[416]

Canadians Debbi Wilkes and Guy Revell started performing "the double twist - both open and closed" in the early 1960s.[417] They were the first Canadian pair to execute a double Lutz twist at the Canadian Championships in Regina in 1963. Wilkes recalled, "We were the first to do double twist and we expanded the Lutz twist - we would do double loop twists as well. That was kind of the first foray into what anyone would have called 'a throw'. We didn't do what would be considered a throw today, but we were the first to do those, which were considered very

---

415 Video footage
416 "The North American Championships", Suzanne Davis King, "Skating" magazine, April 1961
417 Ibid

difficult elements back in those days."[418]

American pairs training under Ron Ludington soon started adding double twist lifts to their programs in the years that followed. Cynthia and Ron Kauffman were doing a split double twist lift as early as 1966.[419] Susie Berens and Roy Wagelein performed the double twist lift at the last World Championships held outdoors in Vienna in 1967.[420]

As twist lifts with more than one revolution became popular, the sport was introduced to a new phenomenon: the 'flea and gorilla' pair.[421] Cynthia and Ron Kauffman's 30-plus centimeter[422] height difference perhaps served as an inspiration for Eastern bloc countries, who started concocting partnerships of skaters with extreme height and weight differences. Notable early examples of these 'flea and gorilla' teams were East Germans Manuela Groß and Uwe Kagelmann and

---
418 Interview with Debbi Wilkes, January 2021
419 Interview with Valerie Jones Bartlett, May 2021
420 "World Championships/Dear Mr. Haines", Dick Button, "Skating" magazine, May 1967
421 "The Winter Olympics: Silver Lining to Comeback, Error delayed Valova recuperation", Beverley Smith, "The Globe and Mail", February 18, 1988
422 "Cindy & Ron: The All American Image", Jane Tarbox, "Skating" magazine, January 1969

Soviets Marina Cherkasova and Sergei Shakhrai. The height and age differences between both teams were startling to many at the time. "Skating" magazine ran an article about Groß and Kagelmann in 1973 with the headline "The Mutt and Jeff Pair", pointing out how their nine-inch height difference helped them accomplish the first triple twist lift and throw double Axel.[423] Groß and Kagelmann's triple twist at the 1970 European Championships in Leningrad may have been a first in international competition.[424]

When they were paired, twelve-year-old Marina Cherkasova and eighteen-year-old Sergei Shakhrai had a thirty-five-centimeter height difference.[425] This extreme (at the time) contrast earned both pairs Olympic medals. Cherkasova and Shakhrai even made their way to the "Guinness Book Of World Records" as the first pairs team in history to perform a quad twist in 1977.[426] The ISU responded to this trend by developing a new

---

423 "The Mutt and Jeff Pair", Dennis L. Bird, "Skating" magazine, March 1973
424 Interview with Frazer Ormondroyd, January 6, 2023; Video footage
425 "Лед в сердце", Evgenia Makarova, "Ogoniok" magazine, May 16-23, 2005
426 "Love of Ice Skating", Howard Bass, 1980

rule that aimed to penalize pairs "when there was a serious imbalance in their physical characteristics, which would lead to an obvious lack of unison."[427] Less than a decade after the rule change, Ekaterina Gordeeva and Sergei Grinkov won their first of 2 Olympic gold medals. The duo had a 28 centimeter height difference.[428]

Lateral twist lifts started showing up in competition in the late 1970s and early 1980s, popularized by pairs like Kitty and Peter Carruthers and Barbara Underhill and Paul Martini.[429] The first mention in "Skating" magazine of a pair performing a double lateral twist was Lorene and Donald Mitchell, at the 1978 Eastern Championships.[430] The triple lateral twist was first popularized by World Champions Isabelle Brasseur and Lloyd Eisler of Canada, who first introduced the move to their program during the 1990/1991 season.[431]

---

427 "Skating Around the World 1892-1992: The One Hundredth Anniversary History of the International Skating Union", Benjamin T. Wright, International Union, 1992
428 "The Winter Olympics: Silver Lining to Comeback, Error delayed Valova recuperation", Beverley Smith, "The Globe and Mail", February 18, 1988
429 Video footage
430 "Easterns", "Skating" magazine, March 1978
431 "The Canadians: Pairs Persistence", Nora McCabe, "The Globe

The twist lift has proved to be a perilous move for many pairs over the years. Cynthia Kauffman broke her ankle practicing the split double twist in 1968.[432] Competitors of two-time Olympic Gold Medallist Aleksandr Zaitsev "said that they had seen slashes on Zaitsev's chest in the dressing room. The marks were from Rodnina's skates cutting him while they were learning the split triple twist lift."[433] Over the years, many male pairs skaters have suffered broken noses from getting elbowed in the face on twists.[434] Timing issues on the entry have resulted in some particularly scary falls. The audience at the Scotiabank Centre in Halifax let out a collective gasp when Kirsten Moore-Towers and Michael Marinaro took a particularly scary fall on their triple twist in the short program at the 2016 Canadian Championships.[435] Despite the riskiness of the element, Skate Canada has described twist lifts as "the most thrilling and exciting

---

and Mail", February 1, 1991
432 "Cindy & Ron: The All American Image", Jane Tarbox, "Skating" magazine, January 1969
433 "The BBC Book of Skating", Sandra Stevenson, 1984
434 Video footage
435 Author's recollection of live event; Video footage

component in pair skating."[436]

---

[436] "Know Your Skating: Glossary", Skate Canada, 2018

Throw Jumps

Long before dazzling throw triple and quad jumps became the gold standard in competitive pairs skating, the flying three jump was considered a novel and rather daring highlight in many pairs teams' programs.

An evolution of hand-in-hand jumping, the long lost sister of side-by-side jumping, the 'flying three jump' (waltz jump) started showing up in pairs programs before World War II. Rosemarie Stewart and Robert S. Dench described "the lady [springing] off the ice and [doing] a flying three-jump, landing on her right-backward-outside edge and joining up with her partner in the waltz position".[437] Maxi Herber and Ernst Baier, the 1936 Olympic Gold Medallists, didn't include the 'flying three jump' in their program, but their Baier Lift[438] was a precursor to the twist or throw loop, without a release.[439]

---

437 "Pair Skating and Dancing on Ice", Rosemarie Stewart and Robert S. Dench, 1943
438 "What's New in Free Skating", Ron Ludington, "Skating" magazine, March 1969
439 Video footage

In the 1950s, Frances Dafoe and Norris Bowden popularized release jumps at a time when several judges claimed these innovations were illegal.[440] Dafoe and Bowden performed the 'flying three jump' (assisted waltz jump), invented the leap of faith and Dafoe even performed an Axel into her partner's arms.[441] By today's standards, it seems like pretty elementary stuff but at the time it was truly groundbreaking and quite controversial, as the ISU didn't permit pairs to do anything overly 'acrobatic' at the time – even overhead lifts where a man fully extended his lifting arm were a no-no.[442]

By the early 1960s, the International Skating Union's rules surrounding throws stated, "If the jumping partner is assisted in the jump by the other partner must consist of one continuous ascending and descending movement."[443]

---

[440] "Canadian Olympic skater Frances Dafoe became a designer to stars", Beverley Smith, "The Globe and Mail", September 30, 2016

[441] "Reflections", Frances Dafoe, "Skating Through Time", February 1998

[442] "Meditation about the future of the World Figure Skating family, ISU - International Skating Union, New Judging System, 'COP for Judges'? The ISU Congress of 2004. Is figure skating an extreme or artistic sport", Ludmila and Oleg Protopopov, 2004

[443] "The Art of Figure Skating", Captain T.D. Richardson, 1962

True throw jumps were popularized later in the 60s by Cynthia and Ron Kauffman of the United States. Their throw single Axel was for a time known simply as 'the Kauffman' or 'the killer'.[444] They staked claim to developing the daring release move with their coach Ron Ludington. Gregory R. Smith noted, "The throw Axel was created in only two lessons. It was conceived during a lesson with Cynthia and Ron Kauffman and matured after in a lesson with Patti Gustafson and Pieter Kollen."[445]

East Germans Heidemarie Steiner and Heinz-Ulrich Walther and Soviets Tatiana Zhuk and Alexander Gorelik also both included the throw single Axel in their free skating routine at the 1968 Olympics.[446] It wasn't until the early 1970s that the first 'recognized' throw double Axel in competition was performed by the East German pair of Manuela Groß and Uwe Kagelmann. They first accomplished the jump in international competition at the 1970 European Championships in Leningrad. At

---

444 "What's New in Free Skating", Ron Ludington, "Skating" magazine, March 1969
445 "Coach of Champions: A Close Look at Ron Ludington", Gregory R. Smith, "Skating" magazine, January 1978
446 Video footage

the 1972 European Championships, Groß and Kagelmann successfully performed not one, but two, throw double Axels.[447] By 1973, two American pairs - Melissa and Mark Militano[448] and Debbie Hughes and Philipp Grout - also successfully executed the throw at the U.S. Championships.[449]

The throw double Axel became a mainstay by the 1970s.[450] Tamara Moskvina and Igor Moskvin noted, "In 1972 only one of the 10 best pairs in the world had a triple twist lift and double Axel throw jump... In 1978 nine pairs were already performing these elements."[451]

It didn't take long for teams to attempt throw triples. Soviets Irina Vorobieva and Aleksandr Vlasov and Julia and Ardo Rennick were among the first teams to attempt a throw triple Salchow in competition.[452] Vorobieva and Vlasov were coached by Stanislav Zhuk

---

447 Interview with Frazer Ormondroyd, January 6, 2023; Video footage
448 "Nationals '72", Josephine Lawless, "Skating" magazine, March 1972
449 "Nationals '73", Sal Zanca, "Skating" magazine, April 1973
450 Video footage
451 "Pair Skating as Sport and Art", Tamara Moskvina and Igor Moskvin, International Skating Union, 1987
452 Video footage

in Moscow, while the Estonian Rennicks were trained by Igor Moskvin in Leningrad. The first Canadian pair to successfully do the throw triple Salchow in competition were Barbara Underhill and Paul Martini, at the 1978 Canadian Championships in Victoria.[453] Ultimately, the first successful throw triple Salchow in international competition was performed by Americans Tai Babilonia and Randy Gardner, students of World Champion John Nicks.[454]

The first pair to attempt a throw triple loop in international competition were Americans Melissa Militano and Johnny Johns, at the 1974 World Championships in Munich, but Melissa fell.[455] The first pair to successfully do the throw triple loop were East Germans Romy Kermer and Rolf Oesterreich, a year later at the European Championships in Copenhagen.[456]

It's interesting to note that Irina Rodnina, who won ten World pairs titles during the same era, didn't routinely include throw jumps in

---

453 "Canadian's", Frank Nowosad, "Skating" magazine, April 1978
454 Video footage
455 "Worlds '74", Howard Bass, "Skating" magazine, May 1974
456 "Europeans", Dennis L. Bird, "Skating" magazine, April 1975

her programs with either of her partners. Sandra Stevenson claimed, "Her second coach, Tatiana Tarasova, said that was inelegant for the man to throw away his partner. In fact, she never tried the moves because of fear of injury."[457]

By the mid-1980s, it was considered standard practice for teams to include a throw triple jump and throw double Axel in their free skating performances.[458] By 1980, the CFSA's Gold Pair Test actually required a throw double Axel.[459] At the 1982 ISU Congress, the regulations of a 'well-balanced program for free skating' in pairs were clearly defined, but it was ultimately decided not to 'cap' the difficulty of throw jumps.[460]

Though the throw triple Salchow was the most popular of the throw triples attempted in the 1980s, East Germans Sabine Baeß and Tassilo Thierbach had a throw triple toe-loop in their repertoire.[461] Their training mates

---
457 "BBC Book of Skating", Sandra Stevenson, 1984
458 Video footage
459 Rulebook, Canadian Figure Skating Association, 1980
460 "Skating Around the World 1892-1992: The One Hundredth Anniversary History of the International Skating Union", Benjamin T. Wright, International Union, 1992
461 "BBC Book of Skating", Sandra Stevenson, 1984

Peggy Seidel and Ralf Seifert also went for the throw triple toe-loop at the 1982 World Junior Championships in Sarajevo but were unsuccessful.[462] Americans Gillian Wachsman and Robert Daw landed the throw triple toe-loop at Skate America in 1983[463] and Soviets Larisa Selezneva and Oleg Makarov attempted the throw in their medal-winning free skate at the 1984 Winter Olympic Games.[464]

One of the first pairs to attempt two throw triple jumps in their free skate were Canadians Cynthia Coull and Mark Rowsom (the Salchow and loop) in 1984.[465] Elena Valova and Oleg Vasiliev also attempted two throw triples - the Salchow and toe-loop - in their free skate at the 1986 World Championships in Geneva.[466]

Rena Inoue, a former singles skater for Japan who teamed up with American John Baldwin Jr. made history by landing the first throw triple Axel in competition at the 2006 U.S.

---

[462] "World Junior Figure Skating Championships '83", Sandra Stevenson, "Ice & Roller Skate" magazine, February 1983
[463] "Skate America 1983: An Organizational Success in Rochester, New York", Howard Bass, "Skating" magazine, December 1983
[464] Video footage
[465] Ibid
[466] Ibid

Figure Skating Championships in St. Louis, Missouri.[467] Today, throw triple jumps of all varieties have weaved their way into the repertoire of the world's top teams.

The throw quad Salchow's history traces back to Wilmington, Delaware in 1983, when Kitty and Peter Carruthers were attempting the dangerous move both in out of a harness with coach Ron Ludington. Kitty was landing the throw three out of five times, and the pair considered including it in their program at the 1984 Olympics but ultimately decided not to take the risk.[468] The Carruthers had the throw triple Salchow in their program as juniors in 1978, around the time Babilonia and Gardner were showing off the daring maneuver as seniors.[469]

Though Tiffany Vise and Derek Trent were the first to successfully land the throw quad Salchow in international competition in 2007[470], Canadians Meagan Duhamel and Eric

---

467 Ibid
468 "Gifted U.S. Skaters Who Fight Back", Neil Amdur, "The New York Times", February 5, 1984
469 "New Englands", Mariann Bourque, "Skating" magazine, February 1978
470 "Warning: Duhamel and Radford tackle quad throw Salchow", Beverley Smith, Bev Smith Writes, October 21, 2014

Radford were the first pair to consistently perform the throw in international competition. True 'pros of the throw', Duhamel and Radford even performed the throw quad Lutz in practice.[471] Whereas jumps, spins and lifts have had a relatively long history, the history of thrilling throws is a relatively new phenomenon that has only really risen to prominence in the last fifty years and in the immortal words of Shania Twain - "up, up, up... it can only go up from here!"

TECHNICAL FIRSTS

'Firsts' completed under the 6.0 system were determined through a review of historical videos, as well as consultation of print sources. A very special thank you to Frazer Ormondroyd for his valuable assistance. For elements completed under the IJS System, a positive GOE was the criteria for inclusion in this list.

Throw double Axel

OLYMPICS: Manuela Groß and Uwe Kagelmann, Melissa and Mark Militano (1972)

---

[471] Video footage

WORLDS: Melissa and Mark Militano (1972)*
EUROPEANS: Manuela Groß and Uwe Kagelmann (1970)
FOUR CONTINENTS: Kristy Sargeant and Kris Wirtz, Tiffany Scott and Philip Dulebohn (1999, free skate)***

Throw triple Salchow

OLYMPICS: Sabine Baeß and Tassilo Thierbach, Kitty and Peter Carruthers (1980)
WORLDS: Tai Babilonia and Randy Gardner (1979)
EUROPEANS: Manuela Mager and Uwe Bewersdorff (1980)
FOUR CONTINENTS: Valérie Saurette and Jean-Sébastien Fecteau, Danielle and Steven Hartsell (1999)***

Throw triple toe-loop

OLYMPICS: Sabine Baeß and Tassilo Thierbach (1984)
WORLDS: Sabine Baeß and Tassilo Thierbach (1981)
EUROPEANS: Sabine Baeß and Tassilo Thierbach (1982)
FOUR CONTINENTS: Vanessa Grenier and Maxime Deschamps (2016)****

Throw triple loop

OLYMPICS: Romy Kermer and Rolf Oesterreich (1976)
WORLDS: undetermined**
EUROPEANS: Romy Kermer and Rolf Oesterreich (1975)
FOUR CONTINENTS: Xue Shen and Hongbo Zhao (1999)***

Throw triple flip

OLYMPICS: Julia Obertas and Sergei Slavnov (2006)
WORLDS: Julia Obertas and Alexei Sokolov (2003)
EUROPEANS: Julia Obertas and Alexei Sokolov (2003)
FOUR CONTINENTS: Kathryn Orscher and Garrett Lucash (2004)

Throw triple Lutz

OLYMPICS: Annabelle Langlois and Cody Hay, Caydee Denney and Jeremy Barrett (2010)
WORLDS: Meagan Duhamel and Craig Buntin (2008)
EUROPEANS: Ksenia Stolbova and Fedor Klimov (2014)
FOUR CONTINENTS: Meagan Duhamel and Craig Buntin (2009)

Throw triple Axel

OLYMPICS: Rena Inoue and John Baldwin Jr. (2006)

Throw quad Salchow

OLYMPICS: Meagan Duhamel and Eric Radford (2018)
WORLDS: Meagan Duhamel and Eric Radford (2016)
EUROPEANS: Yuko Kavaguti and Alexander Smirnov (2015)
FOUR CONTINENTS: Meagan Duhamel and Eric Radford (2015)

*The first known written account of a team performing a throw double Axel at the World Championships was Melissa and Mark Militano at the 1972 World Championships. Though footage of Manuela Groß and

Uwe Kagelmann's free skating performances at the 1970 and 1971 World Championships was not readily available, it is entirely likely that they may have performed the throw double Axel at one of those events.
**Melissa Militano and Johnny Johns attempted a throw triple loop at the 1974 World Championships, but Melissa fell. Romy Kermer and Rolf Oesterreich attempted a throw triple loop at the 1975 World Championships, but Romy two-footed the landing, as did Sabine Baeß and Tassilo Thierbach at the 1979 World Championships. Manuela Mager and Uwe Bewersdorff may have been the first, as they completed the throw successfully at the 1978 World Championships, but footage of pairs events at the World Championships from 1976-1980 is too incomplete to make that determination.
***Based on available video footage of the pairs competition at the 1999 Four Continents Championships. Videos of four short programs were unavailable.
****Complete video footage or judge's sheets of the 1999-2004 pairs competitions at the Four Continents Championships (under the 6.0 system) were unavailable for consultation. Grenier and Deschamps were the first team to receive a positive GOE on this element under the IJS System at this event.
*****Rena Inoue and John Baldwin Jr. landed a throw triple Axel at the 2006 World Championships, but received a negative GOE. Aliona Savchenko and Robin Szolkowy's attempts at the 2012 and 2013 World Championships also received negative GOEs.

The Backflip

Taking off on two feet, a backflip is a backward somersault-type jump that has long been a much-loved staple of professional skating.

'Somersault type jumps' were officially banned by the International Skating Union shortly after7[472] Terry Kubicka performed a 'Purzelbaum rückwärts auf dem Eis' at the 1976 Winter Olympic Games and World Championships and found himself all over the newspapers in Europe[473]. The reasoning for the ban was not only safety-based, as one might suppose. The ISU also viewed the backflip as an acrobatic stunt with no "aesthetic value."[474]

Since the ban, at least two skaters have elected to include the jump in their programs in ISU-eligible competitions. Doug Mattis performed one at the 1991 U.S. Championships in Minneapolis and Surya Bonaly performed one

---
472 "ISU Notes", "Skating" magazine, January 1978
473 "Europa Euphoria", "Skating" magazine, April 1976
474 "Historical Dictionary of Figure Skating", James R. Hines, 2011

at the 1998 Winter Olympic Games in Nagano.[475] Both skaters subsequently turned professional soon after.[476]

Antiquarians have pointed to the 1450 BC Bull-Leaping Fresco from the Palace at Knossos in Crete, now in the collections of the Heraklion Archaeological Museum, as one of the earliest images depicting a backflip-like manoeuver.[477] Though its roots can probably be traced to some form of circus or acrobatic performance, it is impossible to say who performed the first off-ice backflip. Kalpana Seshadri aptly pointed out, "Acrobats are usually anonymous... While dance and sports always lend themselves to nationalistic or cultural appropriations, acrobatic movements have no inherent cultural identity. All over the world, people have walked and continue to walk on tightropes, to defy or play with gravity, juggle, balance and fold their bodies, to defy the norm, to flirt with death. While certain natures and cultures may lay claim to excelling at such acts when they are

---
475 Video footage
476 "The Almanac Of Professional Figure Skating Competitions", Ryan Stevens, May 5, 2021
477 "Bronze Age Representations of Aegean Bull-Leaping", John G. Younger, "American Journal of Archaeology", Vol. 80, No. 2 (Spring, 1976)

institutionalized, no one culture can lay claim as inventor of the cartwheel, the backflip, or balancing on a rope, a pole, and so on."[478]

One of the first skaters purported to do a backflip on skates was a noted turn-of-the-century skater[479] and dentist[480] from Ottawa named Dr. Alexander Martin. In 1944, former Vice-President of the Figure Skating Department of the Amateur Skating Association of Canada[481] John S. MacLean recalled, "Dr. Alex. Martin was a prominent skater for many years. He disliked competitions and preferred to encourage others at the old rink on Slater Street. One of his specialties while skating was a somersault in the air, not a handspring nor a cartwheel, but actually 'un sault perilleux' which few if any of his companions ever attempted."[482]

Backflips made their way into professional skating during World War II. Len and

---

[478] "HumAnimal: Race, Law, Language", Kalpana Seshadri, 2012
[479] "The Hub and the Spokes Or, The Capital and Its Environs", Anson Albert Gard, 1904
[480] "Old Time Stuff", "The Ottawa Citizen", September 1, 1923
[481] "Reflections on the CFSA, 1887-1990: A History of the Canadian Figure Skating Association", Teresa Moore, Canadian Figure Skating Association, 1993
[482] "Early Figure Skating in Canada", John S. MacLean, "Skating" magazine, October 1944

Kenneth Mullen were taught how to skate on Dorr's Pond in Manchester, New Hampshire by their older brother Fred, who was a wiz at acrobatics, tap dancing and skating.[483] They learned how to do the backflip on the snow next to the pond, also working with George Nissen, the inventor of the trampoline[484], to perfect the stunt. Kenneth Mullen broke both of his kneecaps the first time he tried the jump on the ice, but was the first of the Trio to succeed in doing it.[485] In 1941, Len and Kenneth quit their day jobs and formed an acrobatic skating trio with their friend Eddie Raiche. The Hub Trio toured with the Ice Capades[486], and Ice Cycles and appeared on "The Art Linkletter Show".[487] What made the Hub Trio's backflips even more unique was that they sometimes jumped them through giant hoops.[488]

Around the very same time[489] The Hub Trio

---

[483] Interview with Mary Anna Paquette, August 2018
[484] "How The Trampoline Came To Be", David Kindy, "Smithsonian" magazine, March 5, 2020
[485] Interview with Jared Hergenrader, August 2018
[486] "Spins Through Professional Circles", "Skating" magazine, October 1941
[487] Interview with Jared Hergenrader, August 2018
[488] "Spins Through Professional Circles", "Skating" magazine, October 1942
[489] "Neither Sun Nor Desert Wind Shall Keep Los Angeles From

were backflipping it up with the Ice Capades, Adele Inge was performing forward and backward somersaults on skates in shows. Inge toured with Sonja Henie's Hollywood Ice Revue and skated in ice shows at the Hotel New Yorker, Adolphus Hotel in Dallas and Netherland Plaza Hotel in Cincinnati, Ohio.[490] Among her bag of acrobatic tricks was a cartwheel on the ice straight into a backflip.[491]

Several other talented skaters performed backflips on ice in the years that followed, including Centre Theatre ice show star Lloyd 'Skippy' Baxter[492] and Tivoli Circuit skater Sally Richardson[493]. The Kermond Brothers (Eric and Norman), like Richardson, hailed from Australia. After performing as acrobats in Vaudeville-style shows that toured Down Under in the forties, they learned how to translate their act to the ice at Richmond Ice Rink in England[494] and performed backflips in Tom Arnold's famous ice pantomimes[495].

Skating", "Los Angeles Times", November 28, 1938
490 "National Ice Skating Guide", Arthur R. Goodfellow, National Sports Publications, 1946 and 1948 editions
491 Video footage
492 "Hollywood Ice Revue", "Billboard" magazine, December 6, 1952
493 Photographic negatives and prints of the Evening Post newspaper, Alexander Turnbull Library, Wellington, New Zealand
494 "Keep Their Balance", "Brisbane Telegraph", September 22, 1953
495 Programme, "Babes in the Wood on Ice" starring Belita as Robin

In the decades that followed, the backflip has been mastered by a who's who of men's figure skating, including Robin Cousins, Scott Hamilton, Brian Orser, Kurt Browning, Jozef Sabovčík, Philippe Candeloro, Nathan Chen, Robert Wagenhoffer and Shawn Sawyer.[496] Both Cousins and Hamilton had their first lessons in the backflip from Skippy Baxter.[497]

In addition to Adele Inge and Sally Richardson, around a dozen other women have performed the jump over the years. U.S. Open Professional Champions Lori Benton and Rory Flack Burghart both had the backflip in their back of tricks[498], as did five-time European Champion Surya Bonaly, who famously performed the jump on one foot, sometimes in combination with a triple Salchow or toe-loop jump.[499] Bonaly first performed a backflip on ice when she was only twelve years old.[500]

Hood, 1950
496 Video footage
497 Interview with Skippy Baxter for "The Fabulous Ice Age" documentary, 2011; "You Wanna Know How Scott Learned to Backflip on Ice?", How Leaders Lead with David Novak, 2022
498 Video footage
499 Ibid
500 "Ice Abroad: 24th Grand Prix International August 22-25, 1990 St. Gervais, France", Jean-Christophe Berlot, "Skating" magazine,

In 1983, Robin Cousins set a Guinness World Record for the longest backflip on figure skates, clearing 5.48 meters (18 feet).[501] Cousins' record was beaten by Canada's Elladj Baldé in August of 2022, who achieved a distance of 6.10 meters (20 feet). Baldé also set a record in 2022 for the most people backflipped over on ice, clearing three people.[502]

December 1990
501 "2014 Sochi Winter Olympics: A record tour around the figure skating world", Amanda Mochan, Guinness World Records, February 5, 2014
502 Guinness Book of Records, Record Search

IJS Firsts

SINGLES SKATING – JUMPING FIRSTS UNDER THE IJS SYSTEM

Only jumps receiving a 0 or positive GOE were considered when compiling this data. In cases where multiple skaters successfully landed the same jump in the same competition, the starting order was used to determine which skater achieved the jump first.

IJS FIRSTS AT THE OLYMPICS

Triple toe-loop (men's): Evgeni Plushenko (2006, short program)
Triple toe-loop (women's): Tuğba Karademir (2006, short program)
Triple Salchow (men's): Chengjiang Li (2006, free skate)
Triple Salchow (women's): Tuğba Karademir (2006, free skate)
Triple loop (men's): Shawn Sawyer (2006, short program)
Triple loop (women's): Yan Liu (2006, short program)
Triple flip (men's): Shawn Sawyer (2006, short program)
Triple flip (women's): Kimmie Meissner (2006, short program)
Triple Lutz (men's): Daisuke Takahashi (2006, short program)
Triple Lutz (women's): Joannie Rochette (2006, short program)
Triple Axel (men's): Evgeni Plushenko (2006, short program)
Triple Axel (women's): Mao Asada (2010, short program)
Quad toe-loop (men's): Evgeni Plushenko (2006, short program)
Quad toe-loop (women's): Kamila Valieva (2022, team event free skate)
Quad Salchow (men's): Min Zhang (2006, free skate)
Quad Salchow (women's): Kamila Valieva (2022, team event free skate)

Quad loop (men's): Yuma Kagiyama (2022, team event free skate)
Quad loop (women's): none
Quad flip (men's): Shoma Uno (2018, short program)
Quad flip (women's): Anna Shcherbakova (2022, free skate)
Quad Lutz (men's): Dmitri Aliev (2018, short program)
Quad Lutz (women's): Alexandra Trusova (2022, free skate)

IJS FIRSTS AT THE WORLD CHAMPIONSHIPS

Triple toe-loop (men's): Brian Joubert (2005, Qualifying Group B)
Triple toe-loop (women's): Júlia Sebestyén (2005, Qualifying Group B)
Triple Salchow (men's): Brian Joubert (2005, Qualifying Group B)
Triple Salchow (women's): Joannie Rochette (2005, Qualifying Group B)
Triple loop (men's): Brian Joubert (2005, Qualifying Group B)
Triple loop (women's) :Júlia Sebestyén (2005, Qualifying Group B)
Triple flip (men's): Brian Joubert (2005, Qualifying Group B)
Triple flip (women's) :Júlia Sebestyén (2005, Qualifying Group B)
Triple Lutz (men's): Gheorghe Chiper (2005, Qualifying Group B)
Triple Lutz (women's): Joannie Rochette (2005, Qualifying Group B)
Triple Axel (men's): Brian Joubert (2005, Qualifying Group B)
Triple Axel (women's): Mao Asada (2009, free skate)
Quad toe-loop (men's): Stéphane Lambiel (2005, Qualifying Group B)
Quad toe-loop (women's): none
Quad Salchow (men's): Min Zhang (2005, Qualifying Group B)
Quad Salchow (women's): Elizabet Tursynbaeva (2019, free skate)
Quad loop (men's): Yuzuru Hanyu (2017, short program)
Quad loop (women's): none
Quad flip (men's): Nathan Chen (2017, short program)
Quad flip (women's): none*
Quad Lutz (men's): Boyang Jin (2017, short program)
Quad Lutz (women's): Alexandra Trusova (2021, free skate)

IJS FIRSTS AT THE EUROPEAN CHAMPIONSHIPS

Triple toe-loop (men's): Andrei Griazev (2005, short program)
Triple toe-loop (women's): Candice Didier (2005, short program)
Triple Salchow (men's): Lukáš Rakowski (2005, free skate)
Triple Salchow (women's): Bianka Pádár (2005, short program)
Triple loop (men's): John Hamer (2005, free skate)
Triple loop (women's): Kiira Korpi (2005, short program)
Triple flip (men's): Martin Liebers (2005, short program)
Triple flip (women's): Irina Slutskaya (2005, short program)

Triple Lutz (men's): Andrei Griazev (2005, short program)
Triple Lutz (women's): Galina Maniachenko (2005, short program)
Triple Axel (men's): Samuel Contesti (2005, short program)
Triple Axel (women's): Alena Kostornaia (2020, short program)
Quad toe-loop (men's): Stéphane Lambiel (2005, short program)
Quad toe-loop (women's): Alexandra Trusova (2020, free skate)
Quad Salchow (men's): Frédéric Dambier (2006, free skate)
Quad Salchow (women's): Alexandra Trusova (2022, free skate)
Quad loop (men's): Daniel Grassl (2019, short program)
Quad loop (women's): none
Quad flip (men's): Daniel Grassl (2020, free skate)
Quad flip (women's): Anna Shcherbakova (2022, free skate)
Quad Lutz (men's): Alexander Samarin (2019, short program)
Quad Lutz (women's): Anna Shcherbakova (2020, free skate)

IJS FIRSTS AT THE FOUR CONTINENTS CHAMPIONSHIPS

Triple toe-loop (men's): Sean Carlow (2005, short program)
Triple toe-loop (women's): Yukari Nakano (2005, short program)
Triple Salchow (men's): Miguel Angel Moyron (2005, free skate)
Triple Salchow (women's): Chae-Hwa Kim (2005, short program)
Triple loop (men's): Chengjiang Li (2005, short program)
Triple loop (women's): Yan Liu (2005, free skate)
Triple flip (men's): Ben Ferreira (2005, short program)
Triple flip (women's): Jennifer Kirk (2005, short program)
Triple Lutz (men's): Ben Ferreira (2005, short program)
Triple Lutz (women's): Dan Fang (2005, short program)
Triple Axel (men's): Chengjiang Li (2005, short program)
Triple Axel (women's): Mao Asada (2008, free skate)
Quad toe-loop (men's): Daisuke Takahashi (2005, short program)
Quad toe-loop (women's): none
Quad Salchow (men's): Min Zhang (2005, free skate)
Quad Salchow (women's): none
Quad loop (men's): Yuzuru Hanyu (2017, short program)
Quad loop (women's): none
Quad flip (men's): Nathan Chen (2017, short program)
Quad flip (women's) :none
Quad Lutz (men's): Boyang Jin (2016, short program)
Quad Lutz (women's):none

*Anna Shcherbakova and Alexandra Trusova both attempted quad flips at the 2021 World

Championships. Anna's attempt was judged as landing on a quarter turn and she received a negative GOE. Alexandra's attempt received a positive GOE, but was called for an unclear take-off edge.

PAIRS SKATING – JUMPING FIRSTS UNDER THE IJS SYSTEM

IJS FIRSTS AT THE OLYMPICS

Side-by-side triple toe-loops: Qing Pang and Jian Tong (2006, short program)
Side-by-side triple Salchows: Dan and Hao Zhang (2006, short program)
Side-by-side triple loops: Ashley Cain-Gribble and Timothy LeDuc (2022, short program)
Side-by-side triple flips: none
Side-by-side triple Lutzes: Meagan Duhamel and Eric Radford (2014, team event short program)
Throw triple toe-loop: Stacey Kemp and David King (2010, short program)
Throw triple Salchow: Marylin Pla and Yannick Bonheur (2006, short program)
Throw triple loop: Tatiana Volosozhar and Stanislav Morozov (2006, short program)
Throw triple flip: Julia Obertas and Sergei Slavnov (2006, short program)
Throw triple Lutz: Caydee Denney and Jeremy Barrett (2010, short program)
Throw triple Axel: Rena Inoue and John Baldwin Jr. (2006, short program)
Throw quad Salchow: Meagan Duhamel and Eric Radford (2018, free skate)
Triple twist: Dorota Zagórska and Mariusz Siudek (2006, free skate)
Quad twist: Cheng Peng and Hao Zhang (2014, free skate)

IJS FIRSTS AT THE WORLD CHAMPIONSHIPS

Side-by-side triple toe-loops: Marylin Pla and Yannick Bonheur (2005, short program)

Side-by-side triple Salchows: Dan and Hao Zhang (2005, short program)
Side-by-side triple loops: none
Side-by-side triple flips: none
Side-by-side triple Lutzes: Meagan Duhamel and Eric Radford (2013, short program)
Throw triple toe-loop: Olga Beständigová and Jozef Beständig (2005, free skate)
Throw triple Salchow: Diana Rennik and Aleksei Saks (2005, short program)
Throw triple loop: Marylin Pla and Yannick Bonheur (2005, short program)
Throw triple flip: Julia Obertas and Sergei Slavnov (2005, short program)
Throw triple Lutz: Meagan Duhamel and Craig Buntin (2008, short program)
Throw triple Axel: none*
Throw quad Salchow: Meagan Duhamel and Eric Radford (2016, free skate)
Triple twist: Tatiana Volosozhar and Stanislav Morozov (2005, free skate)
Quad twist: Cheng Peng and Hao Zhang (2013, free skate)

IJS FIRSTS AT THE EUROPEAN CHAMPIONSHIPS

Side-by-side triple toe-loops: Tatiana Totmianina and Maxim Marinin (2005, short program)
Side-by-side triple Salchows: Tatiana Totmianina and Maxim Marinin (2005, free skate)
Side-by-side triple loops: none
Side-by-side triple flips: none
Side-by-side triple Lutzes: Valentina Marchei and Ondrej Hotarek (2015, short program)
Throw triple toe-loop: Stacey Kemp and David King (2010, free skate)
Throw triple Salchow: Diana Rennik and Aleksei Saks (2005, short program)
Throw triple loop: Maria Petrova and Alexei Tikhonov (2005, short program)
Throw triple flip: Julia Obertas and Sergei Slavnov (2005, short program)
Throw triple Lutz: Ksenia Stolbova and Fedor Klimov (2014, free skate)
Throw triple Axel: none

Throw quad Salchow: Yuko Kavaguti and Alexander Smirnoff (2015, free skate)
Triple twist: Tatiana Volosozhar and Stanislav Morozov (2005, free skate)
Quad twist: Evgenia Tarasova and Vladimir Morozov (2018, free skate)

IJS FIRSTS AT THE FOUR CONTINENTS CHAMPIONSHIPS

Side-by-side triple toe-loops: Qing Pang and Jian Tong (2005, short program)
Side-by-side triple Salchows: Dan and Hao Zhang (2005, short program)
Side-by-side triple loops: Ashley Cain-Gribble and Timothy LeDuc (2017, short program)
Side-by-side triple flips: none
Side-by-side triple Lutzes: Meagan Duhamel and Eric Radford (2013, short program)
Throw triple toe-loop: Vanessa Grenier and Maxime Deschamps (2016, free skate)
Throw triple Salchow: Elizabeth Putnam and Sean Wirtz (2005, short program)
Throw triple loop: Dan and Hao Zhang (2005, short program)
Throw triple flip: Kathryn Orscher and Garrett Lucash (2005, short program)
Throw triple Lutz: Meagan Duhamel and Craig Buntin (2009, short program)
Throw triple Axel: none
Throw quad Salchow: Meagan Duhamel and Eric Radford (2015, free skate)
Triple twist: Dan and Hao Zhang (2005, free skate)
Quad twist: Wenjing Sui and Cong Han (2012, free skate)

*Rena Inoue and John Baldwin Jr. landed a throw triple Axel at the 2006 World Championships, but received a negative GOE. Aliona Savchenko and Robin Szolkowy's attempts at the 2012 and 2013 World Championships also received negative GOEs.

List of Jumps

The following list of figure skating jumps, is far from complete. Numerous split-type variations and small jumps on C Steps, H Steps, counters, rockers, etc. have been excluded for space. Airborne elements which can be performed from the entries of a number of different jumps, like the Hitch Kick, are also missing from this list.

It is important to consider that many of the jumps on this listing with unknown origins may well have had origins on rollers.

AXEL

Attributions: Axel Paulsen[503]

Take-Off and Landing Edges: RFO-LBO

Toe or Edge: Edge

Rotations: 1 ½

BACK ROCKER JUMP

Attributions: Unknown origins, was already known in 1920s[504]

Take-Off and Landing Edges: RBO-RFO[505]

Toe or Edge: Edge

Rotations: ½

---

[503] "Theorie und Praxis des Kunstlaufes am Eise", Gilbert Fuchs, 1926
[504] "The U.S.F.S.A. Carnival of 1925", Henry S. Musser, Skating magazine, March 1925
[505] "Willy Böckl on Figure Skating", 1937, Willy Böckl

BAIER JUMP (FLYING INSIDE COUNTER JUMP)

Attributions: Ernst Baier[506]

Take-Off and Landing Edges: RFI-LBO[507]

Toe or Edge: Edge

Rotations: 1/2

BALLET JUMP

Attributions: Unknown origins, was already known in 1960s[508]

Take-Off and Landing Edges: RBO-RFI

Toe or Edge: Toe

Rotations: 1/2

BOBRIN-OVER JUMP

Attributions: Igor Bobrin[509]

Take-Off and Landing Edges: RFI-LFO (horizontal twist from lunge)

Toe or Edge: Edge

Rotations: ½ (forward twist)

BOURKEY

Attributions: John 'Misha' Petkevich[510]

Take-Off and Landing Edges: LBI-RBO (counter)

Toe or Edge: Toe

Rotations: 1

---

[506] "Some Jumps at a Glance", Mrs. Lenox Napier, "Skating" magazine, reprinted from "The Skating Times" magazine, March 1936
[507] "Jumps: Description and History", Hildegarde Balmain, Pierre Brunet, "Skating" magazine, 1943
[508] "Figure Skating for Beginners", Dennis L. Bird, 1964
[509] "FISU", William C. Haponski, "Skating" magazine, April 1972
[510] "Bold Bourkey for John Misha", "Sports Illustrated" magazine, January 29, 1968

BOWHILL JUMP (BACK COUNTER)

Attributions: Ian Bowhill[511]

Take-Off and Landing Edges: LBO-RBI[512]

Toe or Edge: Edge

Rotations: 1

BUNNY HOP

Attributions: Unknown origins, was already known in the 1930s[513]

Take-Off and Landing Edges: Left flat-Right toe-LFO[514]

Toe or Edge: Toe

Rotations: 0

COLLEDGE JUMP

Attributions: Cecilia Colledge[515]

Take-Off and Landing Edges:

Toe or Edge: LFO-LBI[516]

Rotations: 1 ½

CZAKÓ JUMP (ROBERTSON JUMP)

Attributions: György Czakó[517]

Take-Off and Landing Edges: RBI-LBO

Toe or Edge: Edge

Rotations: 1

---

511 "Modern Figure Skating", Captain T.D. Richardson, 1938
512 Ibid
513 "Marina Court: A Carnival Number for Twelve Girls", Naomi Slater and Gustave Lussi, "Skating" magazine, February 1937
514 "Sports Illustrated: Figure Skating Championship Techniques", John 'Misha' Petkevich, 1988
515 "Another Collection of Jumps", "Skating" magazine, January 1944
516 Ibid
517 Interview with György Czakó, February 24, 2016

DELAYED AXEL

Attributions: Barbara Jones, Gustave Lussi[518]

Take-Off and Landing Edges: RFO-LBO

Toe or Edge: Edge

Rotations: 1 ½

DREHSPRUNG

Attributions: Gilbert Fuchs[519]

Take-Off and Landing Edges: RFO-LBO

Toe or Edge: Edge

Rotations: 1 ½

DUNN JUMP

Attributions: Jack Dunn[520]

Take-Off and Landing Edges: RBO-LFI[521]

Toe or Edge: Edge

Rotations: ½

FALLING LEAF

Attributions: Unknown origins, was already known in 1980s[522]

Take-Off and Landing Edges: RBO-left toe-RFI[523]

Toe or Edge: Edge

Rotations: 1/2

---

518 "Biographical Sketch of Gustave Lussi", Cecily Morrow
519 "Theorie und Praxis des Kunstlaufes am Eise", Gilbert Fuchs, 1926
520 "System in Jumping", T.P.C. (Pat) Low, in "Modern Figure Skating", Captain T.D. Richardson, 1938
521 Ibid
522 "Creative Ice Skating: Ice Dancing, Freestyle, and Pair Skating", Frances Dorsey, Wendy Williams, 1980
523 "The Complete Book of Figure Skating", Carole Shulman, 2002

153

FLIP (TOE SALCHOW)

Attributions: Montgomery Wilson, Gustave Lussi[524]

Take-Off and Landing Edges: RBI-LBO

Toe or Edge: Toe

Rotations: 1

HALF-FLIP

Attributions: Unknown origins, was already known in 1940s[525]

Take-Off and Landing Edges: RBI-LFI/RFO

Toe or Edge: Toe

Rotations: ½

HALF-LOOP (EULER)

Attributions: Gustav and/or Karl Euler[526], Per Thorén[527]

Take-Off and Landing Edges: RBO-LBI

Toe or Edge: Edge

Rotations: 1

HALF-LUTZ

Attributions: Unknown origins, was already known in 1930s[528]

Take-Off and Landing Edges: RBO-LFI/RFO

Toe or Edge: Toe

Rotations: ½

---

524 "Biographical Sketch of Gustave Lussi", Cecily Morrow
525 "Evaluation of Errors in Figures", United States Figure Skating Association, 1945
526 "Gillis Grafström – the Artist among the Figure Skaters", Volker Kluge, "Journal of Olympic History", 2018
527 "Theorie und Praxis des Kunstlaufes am Eise", Gilbert Fuchs, 1926
528 "Some Jumps at a Glance", Mrs. Lenox Napier, "Skating" magazine, reprinted from "The Skating Times" magazine, March 1936

HALF-SCHÄFER JUMP (ONE-FOOT TOELESS LUTZ)
Attributions: Unknown origins, was already known in 1930s[529]
Take-Off and Landing Edges: RBO-RBI[530]
Toe or Edge: Edge
Rotations: 1

HALF-SPLIT LUTZ
Attributions: Unknown origins, was already known in 1970s[531]
Take-Off and Landing Edges: RBO-LFI
Toe or Edge: Toe
Rotations: ½

INSIDE AXEL
Attributions: Willy Böckl[532]
Take-Off and Landing Edges: RFI-RBO
Toe or Edge: Edge
Rotations: 1 ½

INSIDE THREE JUMP (INSIDE JUMPED THREE)
Attributions: Unknown origins
Take-Off and Landing Edges: RFI-RBO
Toe or Edge: Edge
Rotations: ½

---

529 Ibid
530 "Another Collection of Jumps", Megan Taylor, "Skating" magazine, January 1944
531 "ABC voor de Schaatssport", Piet Bergstrom, 1971
532 "Jumps: Description and History", Hildegarde Balmain, Pierre Brunet, "Skating" magazine, 1943.

KADETTENSPRUNG

Attributions: Phil Taylor[533]

Take-Off and Landing Edges: LFO-RFI- RBO (triple jump on ice)[534]

Toe or Edge: Edge

Rotations: ½

LOOP

Attributions: Werner Rittberger[535]

Take-Off and Landing Edges: RBO-RBO

Toe or Edge: Edge

Rotations: 1

LUTZ

Attributions: Alois Lutz[536]

Take-Off and Landing Edges: RBO-LBO

Toe or Edge: Toe

Rotations: 1

MAZURKA

Attributions: Unknown origins, was already known in 1930s[537]

Take-Off and Landing Edges: RBO-LFO

Toe or Edge: Toe

Rotations: ½

---

533 "Eissport", "Linzer Tages-Post", March 6, 1927
534 "Die Schules des Eislaufes", O. Kaetterer, 1935
535 "Faszination Eissport: 100 Jahre Eissport", Heinz Maegerlein, 1986
536 "Neuentdeckungen über Alois Lutz", Dr. Matthias Hampe, "Pirouette" magazine, July/August 2022
537 "Lifts as a Highlight of Pair Skating", Richard L. Hapgood, "Skating" magazine, January 1934

ONE-AND-A-HALF FLIP

Attributions: Unknown origins, was already known in 1930s[538]

Take-Off and Landing Edges: RBI-RFO

Toe or Edge: Toe

Rotations: 1 ½

ONE-AND-A-HALF LUTZ

Attributions: Unknown origins, was already known in the 1930s

Take-Off and Landing Edges: RBO-RFO

Toe or Edge: Toe

Rotations: 1 ½

ONE-FOOT AXEL

Attributions: Ernst Oppacher[539]

Take-Off and Landing Edges: RFO-RBI

Toe or Edge: Edge

Rotations: 1 ½

ONE-FOOT SPLIT AXEL

Attributions: Likely a Gustave Lussi invention[540]

Take-Off and Landing Edges: RFO-RBI

Toe or Edge: Edge

Rotations: 1 ½

---

538 "Maribel Y. Vinson's Advanced Figure Skating", Maribel Vinson Owen, 1940
539 "Sports Illustrated Figure Skating: Championship Techniques", John 'Misha' Petkevich, 1988
540 Video footage

ONE-FOOT LUTZ

Attributions: Unknown origins, was already known in the 1970s[541]

Take-Off and Landing Edges: RBO-RBI

Toe or Edge: Toe

Rotations: 1

ONE-FOOT SALCHOW

Attributions: Unknown origins, was already known in the 1960s[542]

Take-Off and Landing Edges: RBI-RBI

Toe or Edge: Edge

Rotations: 1

PAT LOW

Attributions: Pat Low[543]

Take-Off and Landing Edges: RBI-LBI

Toe or Edge: Edge

Rotations: 1

SALCHOW

Attributions: Ulrich Salchow[544]

Take-Off and Landing Edges: RBI-LBO

Toe or Edge: Edge

Rotations: 1

---

541 "Single Figure Skating for Beginners and Champions, Josef Dědič", 1975
542 "1967 Canadian Championships", Brian Pound, "Skating" magazine, April 1967
543 "Krasobruslení", Vladimir Koudelka, 1936
544 "Handbok i konståkning på skridskor", Ulrich Salchow, 1906

SCHÄFER JUMP (TOELESS LUTZ, DIESEL LUTZ)

Attributions: Karl Schäfer[545]

Take-Off and Landing Edges: RBO-LBO[546]

Toe or Edge: Edge

Rotations: 1

SPLIT FALLING LEAF

Attributions: Unknown origins, was already known in 1980s[547]

Take-Off and Landing Edges: RBO-left toe-RFI[548]

Toe or Edge: Edge

Rotations: ½

SPLIT FLIP

Attributions: Unknown origins, was already known in the 1950s[549]

Take-Off and Landing Edges: RBI-LBO

Toe or Edge: Toe

Rotations: 1

---

545 "Another Collection of Jumps", Clarence Hislop, "Skating" magazine, January 1944
546 "Some Jumps at a Glance", Mrs. Lenox Napier, "Skating" magazine, reprinted from "The Skating Times" magazine, March 1936
547 "Creative Ice Skating: Ice Dancing, Freestyle, and Pair Skating", Frances Dorsey, Wendy Williams, 1980
548 Ibid
549 "Easterns", Joseph P. Gibson, "Skating" magazine, April 1950

SPLIT JUMP/RUSSIAN SPLIT JUMP

Attributions: Unknown origins, was already known in 1930s[550]

Take-Off and Landing Edges: LBI-RFI

Toe or Edge: Toe

Rotations: ½

SPLIT LUTZ

Attributions: Lloyd 'Skippy' Baxter[551]

Take-Off and Landing Edges: RBO-LBO

Toe or Edge: Toe

Rotations: 1

SPREAD EAGLE JUMP (MONDSPRUNG)[552]

Attributions: E.T. Goodrich[553]

Take-Off and Landing Edges: LFO and RFO spread eagle-RFO and LFO spread eagle[554]

Toe or Edge: Edge

Rotations: 1

STAG JUMP

Attributions: Karl Schäfer[555]

Take-Off and Landing Edges: RBI-LFI

Toe or Edge: Toe

Rotations: ½

---

550 "Some Jumps at a Glance", Mrs. Lenox Napier, "Skating" magazine, reprinted from "The Skating Times" magazine, March 1936
551 "Sheldon Galbraith, The Early Years", PJ Kwong and Mel Matthews, "Skating Through Time", July 1998
552 "Das Eissport-Buch", Fritz Reuel, 1928
553 "The Skater's Text Book", Marvin R. Clark and Frank Swift, 1868
554 Ibid
555 "Hints to Skaters", Mary Rose Thacker, "Skating" magazine, December 1940

TAFFY JUMP (FORWARD INSIDE LOOP)

Attributions: Taffy Pergament[556]

Take-Off and Landing Edges: RFI-RFI[557]

Toe or Edge: Edge

Rotations: 1

THREE JUMP (JUMPED THREE)

Attributions: Unknown

Take-Off and Landing Edges: RFO-RBI

Toe or Edge: Edge

Rotations: ½

TOE SPLIT LOOP

Attributions: Unknown origins, was already known in the 1950s[558]

Take-Off and Landing Edges: RBO-RBO

Toe or Edge: Toe

Rotations: 1

TOE WALLEY

Attributions: Unknown origins, was already known in the 1940s[559]

Take-Off and Landing Edges: RBI-RBO

Toe or Edge: Toe

Rotations: 1

---

556 "A Jump In Search Of A Name", Astrid Hagenguth, "Skating" magazine, February 1967
557 Ibid
558 "United States Championships", Sevy Von Sonn, "Skating" magazine, May 1954
559 "The Championships of Canada", Catherine Gillies, "Skating" magazine, April 1949

TOE-LOOP (CHERRY FLIP)

Attributions: Bruce Mapes[560]

Take-Off and Landing Edges: RBO-RBO

Toe or Edge: Toe

Rotations: 1

TUCK AXEL

Attributions: Unknown origins, was already known in 1970s[561]

Take-Off and Landing Edges: RFO-LBO

Toe or Edge: Edge

Rotations: 1 ½

UNNAMED JUMP

Attributions: Gustav Hügel[562]

Take-Off and Landing Edges: RFI-RBO[563]

Toe or Edge: Edge

Rotations: 1 ½

UNNAMED JUMP

Attributions: Ulrich Salchow

Take-Off and Landing Edges: LBO-RFI[564]

Toe or Edge: Edge

Rotations: ½

---

560 "Sports Illustrated Figure Skating: Championship Techniques", John 'Misha' Petkevich, 1988
561 "ABC Presents...", Virginia Gilley, "Skating" magazine, April 1971
562 "System in Jumping", T.P.C. (Pat) Low, in "Modern Figure Skating", Captain T.D. Richardson, 1938
563 Ibid
564 "A Handbook of Figure Skating Arranged For Use On The Ice", George Henry Browne, 1907

WALLEY

Attributions: Nate Walley[565], Pat Low[566], Hugo Distler[567]

Take-Off and Landing Edges: RBI-LBO

Toe or Edge: Edge

Rotations: 1

WALTZ JUMP (THREE JUMP)

Attributions: Unknown origins, earliest mention in print is in Garcin's 1813 book "Le Vrai Patineur"[568]

Take-Off and Landing Edges: RFO-LBO

Toe or Edge: Edge

Rotations: ½

WILSON JUMP

Attributions: J. Wilson[569]

Take-Off and Landing Edges: LBO-RBO (rockerwise)[570]

Toe or Edge: Edge

Rotations: 1

---

565 "Turner's Turn", Eugene Turner, "Skating" magazine, April 1984
566 "Maribel Y. Vinson's Advanced Figure Skating", Maribel Vinson Owen, 1940
567 "The Art of Jumping: A Spectator's Guide – II: Jumps from a Backward Edge", Dennis L. Bird (writing under pseudonym John Noel), "Skating World" magazine, February 1961
568 "Le Vrai Patineur, ou principes sur l'art de patiner avec grace", Jean Garcin, 1813
569 "System in Jumping", T.P.C. (Pat) Low, in "Modern Figure Skating", Captain T.D. Richardson, 1938
570 "Some Jumps at a Glance", Mrs. Lenox Napier, "Skating" magazine, reprinted from "The Skating Times" magazine, March 1936

163

WREDE JUMP

Attributions: Ludwig Wrede[571]

Take-Off and Landing Edges: RBO-LFO[572]

Toe or Edge: Edge

Rotations: 1 ½

---

[571] "Jumps: Description and History", Walter Arian, "Skating" magazine, 1943
[572] Ibid

IJS Jump Base Values

The IJS System – or "the new system" as curmudgeons like me still call it in 2023 – is based on the premise that each jump is worth a certain value, to which the jump is analyzed and assigned a positive or negative Grade of Execution.

As the International Skating Union's Communication No. 2475 (Scale of Values for the 2022/23 Season in Single & Pair Skating) reads like a stereo system manual from the 1980s, this simplified little chart might prove a handy reference the next time doing mental math as you watch the world's most exciting sport.

Jump	Value
Double Toe-Loop	1.3
Double Salchow	1.3
Double Loop	1.7
Double Flip	1.8
Double Lutz	2.1
Double Axel	3.3
Triple Toe-Loop	4.2
Triple Salchow	4.3
Triple Loop	4.9
Triple Flip	5.3
Triple Lutz	5.9
Triple Axel	8
Quad Toe-Loop	9.5
Quad Salchow	9.7
Quad Loop	10.5

Quad Flip	11
Quad Lutz	11.5
Quad Axel	12.5
Double Twist	2.6-3.4 (based on level)
Triple Twist	4.8-6.0 (based on level)
quad Twist	6.4-8.0 (based on level)
Throw Double Toe-Loop	2.5
Throw Double Salchow	2.5
Throw Double Loop	2.8
Throw Double Flip	3
Throw Double Lutz	3
Throw Double Axel	4
Throw Triple Toe-Loop	4.4
Throw Triple Salchow	4.4
Throw Triple Loop	5
Throw Triple Flip	5.3
Throw Triple Lutz	5.3
Throw Triple Axel	6
Throw Quad Toe-Loop	6.5
Throw Quad Salchow	6.5
Throw Quad Loop	7
Throw Quad Flip	7.5
Throw Quad Lutz	7.5
Backflips	0*

Mandatory 2 point deduction if identified by the Technical Specialist and decided a majority of the Technical Panel

Acknowledgments

A warm and very special thank you to the following people for their contributions to the research behind this book:

Valerie (Jones) Bartlett
Linda Carbonetto Villella
György Czakó
Meagan Duhamel
Gordon Forbes
Dr. Matthias Hampe
Doug Haw
Elaine Hooper
Jay Humphry
Barb and Don Jackson
Doug Leigh
Kerry Leitch
Allison Manley
John McKilligan
Frazer Ormondroyd
Mary Petrie McGillvray
Mark Rowsom
Bob Turk†
Tina Tyan
Jean Westwood†
Debbi Wilkes
Benjamin T. Wright†

A Note From The Author

Thank you so much for your support and kind interest!

I hope that you have enjoyed reading "Technical Merit: A History of Figure Skating Jumps" as much as I enjoyed writing it.

If so, I would so appreciate it if you took a few moments to write a short, honest review on the retailer's site where you purchased your copy, as well as popular book review sites.

Reviews can make such a <u>huge difference</u> in this important history reaching the hands of more people.

Other Books

Sequins, Scandals & Salchows: Figure Skating in the 1980s

Jackson Haines: The Skating King

The Almanac of Canadian Figure Skating

A Bibliography of Figure Skating

www.ingramcontent.com/pod-product-compliance
Lightning Source LLC
LaVergne TN
LVHW051600070426
835507LV00021B/2688